The Curriculum Framework

I am indebted to Francis Reid, the British Lighting Designer, for his very practical approach to solving stage lighting problems. He asks himself "If I had one lighting instrument, where would I hang it? If I had two, where would I hang them? If three?" and so on.

If I had one course to offer in Theatre what would it be? If ever given the opportunity for two, or three, or four? Here are my suggestions:

The first course should be Theatre Fundamentals, a survey/introductory class; a potpourri of all theatre has to offer. I have found it very helpful to give out a survey form on the first day of class to find out what area of theatre students are most interested in. But all areas should be covered, regardless. I am a strong believer in the idea that all actors should be technicians at one time or another, and all techies should perform. Ensemble becomes more apparent when backstage people can be empathetic with the problems of performing and vice versa.

The second course would be an advanced acting class called Character Portrayal. A majority of the people I have worked with in theatre want to be an actor, or at least know more about Acting. The performance exercises in this class are a bit more complicated and there is more work to do in this intensive semester class.

The third course would be Design. This class would be divided into two halves – one devoted to learning the skills required in technical theatre, the second, an introduction to all aspects of theatre design – Set, Lights, Costume, and Sound.

The fourth course would be Theatre Performance. The focus would be exclusively towards producing and performing a show.

This class could be repeatable, and the choice of show would be determined by the size, gender, the work ethic of the class.

The fifth course would be Independent Study in Theatre. This is where a student takes over all aspects of production – whether they choose acting, directing, stage management or design.

I personally prefer my theatre classes to be 1½ hour long 3 times a week. You need that time to set the days goals, get participants warmed up, get into the "groove," (15 minutes) work/perform, lesson/critique (65 minutes), and then wind down, which includes taking deep gasping breaths, summarizing the day's activities and possibly handing out home work. (10 minutes).

Values of a lesson plan:

I believe in lesson plans. You may or may not use them religiously, but having guidelines during the course of a teaching day is very important. Focus, being succinct, outcome-oriented are but of the few benefits of a well-made lesson plan.

Here's a basic template for a day's work in a class:

____

Teacher

____

Class Name and Date

____

Today's Objective:

____

Exercises to reach the objective:

____

Examples of seeing the objective reached:

____

Summary

Classroom Critique

It is best that you give feedback as a teacher early on, so that students can understand how to do it. By the second classroom exercise, get the rest of the class involved.

Participants should always have a computer, pencil, notebook or a blank sheet ready for writing down classroom critique.

1) Comments are not judgments - "I would have done it this way" "I didn't believe that" "That was wrong"

2) Comments are about what the participants saw, heard and felt in the performance – "I saw you doing this – is this what you were trying to do?" "I felt this kind of emotion when you did this" "I was a bit confused by this action that you did – were you doing this?"

3) After everyone has given comments, the player then explains what he was trying to do. The suggestions can then come from participants as to another way of trying it so that the action or the feeling would have been better communicated.

Participants giving feedback should be constructive. Choose words carefully, especially when a class is new to this method of critique. It will get easier to do over time.

> Feedback is huge. I would say seventy percent of what I do (probably more) as a teacher is give feedback. My feedback never stops, unless a student tells me to stop. I write feedback about students I taught years ago when I watch them on the stage (I bring this little notebook, and my former students say "there's Palmore and his notebook again...") I don't give it to them unless they ask for it, and most of them do. I'm grateful for that learning ethic in them.

Acting Class Terminology

Coach – the role the teacher plays when training exercises are being done. The goal of a coach is to keep focus on what the exercise is for, rather than the "game" often associated with improvisation.

> I was probably a nuisance as an acting student. I didn't like doing an improvisation unless I knew why I was doing it. Like a little kid Palmore was always asking "why are we doing this exercise?" I still assess improvisations that way to this day. It can't be just a game, it has to have justification in the training of an actor. Some improvisations are just fun and meaningless, and end up being class distractions. Bah humbug.

Exercises – are classroom presentations. There are two types – Classroom Performance Exercises, which are graded, and critiqued. Classroom Training Exercises, which are skill centered warm-ups and improvisations.

Projects – are student's homework that are performed for and critiqued by the class.

Participants – are essentially the students in the class. The participant becomes the "Player" when he is personally doing an exercise in front of everyone else.

> I will occasionally slip with terminology, calling a participant a student, learner or an actor. I hope you get it, it is not meant to confuse. The term just looked right at the time.

Theatre Fundamentals

The first day:

Introduce yourself. Have students introduce themselves.

Hand out a syllabus (sample is given), and go over items one by one. Especially emphasize deadlines. NO LATE WORK.

Establish the classroom environment and routine. Goals for the day, warmups, exercises, summary.

> I firmly believe in joining in all class **warmups** you have students do. None of this "you do, I'll watch" for this portion. The idea is that "if the teacher is silly, I guess I can be. It's safe to do so."
> **Exercises** are slightly different in that you start the exercise going by giving an example, and then pull back to let them do it, coaching and encouraging along the way.

First day Warmup/exercise

1. Three things – have each person pick a pair. Through a series of questions, give them three minutes to find out three things they have in common. NOT like "we're both male, both have mothers, etc. but something unique like "we found out our brothers are both left handed" "we found out we went to the same preschool." At the end, have people share unusual things in common.

2. "You look at us, we look at you." Split the class into two groups – one audience, one "performers." Have performers stand in a straight line facing the audience. Have audience observe the performers. Do it as long as possible. You will notice shifting, giggles, unnecessary movement. Then give the performers something to do – such as counting the floorboards in the room, number of chairs and so on. Have a small discussion with both groups after this simple yet essential exercise: The lesson here is Acting is about **doing**.

As a teacher your goal is to build trust, confidentiality, encouragement, play and good work ethic.

Early on – exercises on audience perception

One of the prevalent problems of actors is the inability to perceive how an audience hears and sees them while they are onstage. An easy method to solve this is to view video tapes of their performances. The downside of that is that video tape rarely shows the actual "feel" of a performance.

There are two issues to resolve: communication through sound, and communication through sight.

Communication through sound.

Does the actor know how loud or how soft and articulate he needs to be to fill a particular performance space? An audience doesn't really hear an actor until it feels that the actor has filled the space with sound - that is, that the sound is strong and complete. If it is too high, or too low in pitch, the audience will say "we can't hear you" even though volume and clarity is fine. On the other hand, the audience will say the same if the sound is full, yet lacking in volume and clarity.

Solutions: 1) expansion of vocal range
                  2) better breathing habits, or better breathing control.

Exercise in a theatre space: Have class seat themselves all over a theatre audience. Have students come up one by one and read aloud a selected monologue or newspaper article. Have audience members raise their hands if they cannot understand them. Do this exercise later on in the semester, when students have a had a bit of vocal work on articulation and projection. See if there is progress.

Communication through sight

Does the actor know what he looks like to the audience? Not physical appearance, but what the performer is saying with his/her body? Again, watching a video or looking at the mirror while working on a monologue is good (and humbling), but the actor needs to know if the body is conveying what he thinks he is communicating.

PUNAHOU THEATRE
COURSE SUMMARY
SCHOOL YEAR 2010-2011

COURSE TITLE: THEATRE FUNDAMENTALS   **Palmore**: 943-3673
Semester (Not Repeatable), Prerequisite: None

No previous experience is necessary. The emphasis of this course is to introduce the young person to the world of acting. Realistic Theatre, Acting "Methods," Greek Theatre, and Shakespeare are but a few of the topics covered in this course. Activities include theatre games, pantomime, and improvisation.

COURSE OBJECTIVES:
The learner will be introduced to important Theatre concepts that are essential in understanding how the magic of Theatre occurs. These include, but are not limited to:

1. ENSEMBLE	9. THE EXPANDED VOICE
2. CHARACTERIZATION	10. THE EXPANDED BODY
3. THEME	11. PLOT
4. IMPULSE	12. DIALOGUE
5. IMPETUS	13. SPECTACLE
6. IMPROVISATION	14. ACOUSTICS
7. THE NEUTRAL BODY	16. WORD COLORING
8. THE NEUTRAL VOICE	16. STAGE BLOCKING

The learner will apply these concepts in various class exercises that will also introduce or improve these skills:

1. PROPER BREATHING	5. BODY, VOICE VERSATILITY
2. PANTOMIME	6. "METHOD" ACTING
3. VOICE PROJECTION	7. "TECHNICAL" ACTING
4. VOICE ARTICULATION	

TEXT: <u>AN ACTOR'S HANDBOOK</u>
               <u>MAKE THEATRE HAPPEN: Acting and Directing</u>:
               Paul Palmore.

STUDENT RESPONSIBILITIES/CLASS REQUIREMENTS:

1. Being on time and attending class daily.
2. Active involvement in classroom exercises.
3. **Attendance and Reaction Paper to a Theatre Production.**
   A reaction paper should be written about all aspects of the production - a handout is provided for guidance. **1,000 Word Minimum.**
4. Graded Individual and Group Projects, each receiving a grade of thirty points.
5. **The People Portfolio. Three people in the 1st quarter. (Ten points each, 30 points total)**
6. **"Through Someone Else's Eyes" acting project and documentation, due the middle of the 2nd quarter. (30 points)**
7. Loose clothes for acting work.
8. **The final review exam. (60 points)**

STUDY HELP:

Study help is available to all theatre students during Palmore's office hours. Students need to make an appointment for study help sessions, as rehearsals and set construction are often done during these periods. The type of study help you may need may include any of the following:

1. Help with blocking and interpretation of an acting scene.
2. Questions about any discussion or lecture.
3. Questions about interpretation of a scene from a Theatre presentation.
4. Help with class project work.

GRADING PROCEDURES:

Grades in this class are based on awarding points for work done in and out the classroom and is generally divided into 4 separate equally weighted categories each quarter.

As an example:

 1st Quarter

People Watching Exercise	30 points
Storytelling Exercise	30 points
Classroom Exercises/Activities	30 points
Acting Monologues	30 points

Students may be able to find out their grade by consulting through the grading sheet posted after each exercise, or by emailing Palmore.

Extra credit may be earned in all Theatre classes by helping PUNAHOU THEATRE events.

<u>TENTATIVE SYLLABUS FOR THIS SEMESTER:</u>

Introduction   Syllabus, A few things I'd like you to know

<u>Areas of Study</u>

<u>ACTING</u>

	Handouts -	The Stanislavski System Meyerhold People Watching Form
	Exercises -	In class Acting Exercises
	Projects -	1) People Watching 2) Storytelling 3) Monologues

<u>TECHNICAL THEATRE</u>

	Exercises	Theatre Tour Lighting Demonstration The Theme Park Exercise Design the Emotion exercise

<u>REALISTIC THEATRE</u>

	Handouts -	Six rehearsal phases
	Project -	Scene from The Crucible

<u>THEATRE PRODUCTION</u>

	Project -	Final Theatre Presentations

SAMPLE INFORMATION SHEET

(a template for how to make an information sheet...)

NAME: ID NO:

GRADE: Cell #

HEIGHT

AFTER SCHOOL STUFF: (such as work, athletics, dance, singing)

VOCAL RANGE:

MUSICAL INSTRUMENTS:

PREVIOUS THEATRE EXPERIENCE

THINGS YOU'D LIKE TO DO IN THIS THEATRE CLASS
(Something you haven't done before, something you'd like to find out about)

I: Acting Project One: The People Watching Exercise

Why we do it: To learn the practical as well as aesthetic decisions and processes used in characterization. Real people are the actor's library. We learn voices, mannerisms, new movement patterns, new facial expressions from the people we meet on the street. While this is the first exercise I give, it is timeless – whenever I see an actor fumbling with creating his character, I tell him to get back to basics and watch people!

> The first person I wrote in my portfolio about was written 30 minutes after this assignment was given me in an acting class in 1972. I finally used the mannerisms and voice (but with an Italian accent) 32 years later playing old Salieri in "Amadeus." You just never know when you're going to need that person you wrote about!

How assessed: Through a presentation of a two-minute monolog of a person observed. When the performance is done, participants in class critique the work.

This assignment is given two weekends in advance of performance. Players are asked to observe people in the street, at a bus stop, in an airport, in the classroom, at home, on the bus, at the park, in a restaurant. Hand out at least two documentation forms per student, or send as a writable pdf.

Their people are performed for the entire class.
Requirements:
1. The performance must be at least two minutes long, so as to give enough time to observe their work. Their "people" may or may not talk, depending upon the encounter they had with their person.
2. The player hands in the people watching form when he performs. You will often note that the detail in the written work shows up in the detail of a performance.
3. The player describes where he observed his person to the class. He does not describe his person at all, to the point of not saying whether his person is male or female. He may describe a prop he is using if he doesn't have the actual prop.
4. He mentally gets ready for the performance, not rushing into it. He calls "curtain" to indicate to his audience that he has started the performance.
5. He performs, then calls "curtain" at the end of his performance.
6. The rest of the class gives critique. You as teacher have final say. Critique shouldn't be more than 5 minutes per performer.

Teacher: Spend about twenty minutes in class going over these categories. After that, have participants work in pairs observing each other. See if they can perform each other after they practice.

1. <u>Movement through space</u> - Imagine that the space around the person you are observing is very thick, like a bowl of jello. How does the person move through the space in front of him? Verbs like push, cut, slice, smash, glide, slide are but a few examples. This does not mean that the whole body moves through space the same way. The chest may "slice" while the arms "smash". It is best to observe the chest, arms, legs, and head primarily.

2. <u>Rooted or lifted</u> - that is, is the weight of the body pushed down, or does it seem lifted up in the air? Again, some people have heavy, plodding, "rooted" feet, while having lifted chests. Observe how bodies react when every step is taken.

3. <u>Leading body part</u> - Many people lead with their chests, some with their waists, others with their heads, and a lot of people change what they lead with over time, or they lead differently in different emotional states. The question to ask is: if the person were a pull toy, what part of the body would you attach the string to?

4. <u>Mask</u> - how is the face "held"? People hold their faces in many different ways - a scowl, a smile, a frown, an almost mindless blank. Make a crude drawing, get a digital picture if you can, or describe it.

5. <u>Standing Attitude</u> - How does the body come to rest when standing? You can draw a stick figure, get a pic, or describe.

6. <u>Sitting Attitude</u> - How does the body come to rest when sitting? An important note is whether a person is relaxed or not - sitting attitudes change dramatically with different emotions.

7. <u>Arms and Hands</u> - how does the person use their hands?

8. <u>Voice</u> - Note the characteristics by these criteria:

Pitch - high, medium, low   Speed - Fast, medium, slow
Volume - loud, medium, soft   Timbre - Harsh, medium, smooth

Also note quirks a person might have: a lisp, an accent.

9. <u>Mannerisms, deformities, scars</u> - nervous twitches, brushing hair out of face, a limp, a tattoo, a scar on the cheek.

10. <u>Mind</u> – this part is optional. I like it because I try and tell a story to determine why the person is who he is. What is he thinking? How did he get this way? It's fictional storytelling using the imagination.

11. <u>Costume</u> - what is the person wearing? Many actors can get into character simply by the clothes they wear, and people have the funny habit of changing their personalities based on their clothing. Drawings or detailed descriptions (digital pictures/video is best!) are needed here.

(a template)

Name

Movement   **Character name**

Movement through space | rooted or lifted | leading body part
                         | | |
                         | | |

The Persona

Standing attitude

(areas to be filled in)

Sitting attitude

Arms and hands

Face

Voice

pitch - high, medium, low   speed - fast, medium, slow
volume - loud, medium, soft   timbre - harsh, medium, smooth

Accent, lisp, vocal mannerism?

Mind

Costume

I: Acting Project Two: The Storytelling exercise

This might seem easy, but I find most of my actors need to learn how to tell a story, and need this introductory exercise to help them along. They seem to have a grip on creating characters and maybe, memorizing lines, but neglect the most important aspect of theatre, and that is telling a story their own personal way.

The requirements of the exercise:

1. A four to seven-minute story. It does not have to be memorized, though many of my students find it easier to perform it that way. However, the story cannot be read verbatim.
2. A storybook with pictures may be used. The most successful have been Dr. Seuss books, with Mother Goose, Grimm's fairy tales coming in a close second.
3. A human-interest story may be told. Not a personal one, but the "chicken soup" books have been very successful in the classroom. The danger of personal ones is that they become quite emotional, and the storyteller stops being objective. I've had crying fests in the classroom, and try being the performer after that!
4. Ghost stories are very successful. It seems that half of a class always has a scary story they want to tell, complete with great characters and interesting sound effects. Edgar Allen Poe works quite well.
5. There are great sources for good stories on the Internet, though many of them are terribly long and need editing.

Some tips for telling a good story.

1. The effective use of silence for suspense. Often followed with the "jump" moment of the story.
2. A good outline.
3. Practicing at home. Or with friends. Not making the classroom the first attempt.
4. A storybook with BIG pictures.
5. Clear articulation for the narrator/storyteller.
6. Effective use of accents, or change of pitch, duration, volume, timbre, to create characters.
7. Communion with the audience – through eye contact, careful display of the picture book to the entire class, and checking to see if the story is coming along well. You don't have this luxury as an actor, but it is vital to a storyteller.

Treat this exercise with respect. And impose this respect for effective storytelling to your actors. A storyteller is theatre in its most minimal form. If you can't tell a story, you can't act. It's that simple.

Another important part of this exercise is stressing to the actor that he must really want to tell this story. Anything less than that total commitment makes it awful for the audience. This leads to the bigger analogy of a director and his cast being totally committed to a play being told in their personal way.

It is important to set the tone for each story told. I personally like to set up a chair in front of the class, and use a spotlight slightly front and to the left or right of the performer (white light) with a blue backlight behind the performer. If you have a dimmer handy, brighten the lights for jokes and lighter stuff, darken for the scary material. If no special lights, at least have a semi-circle of chairs around the storyteller, maybe 3-4 feet away for the audience. P.s It is not necessary that the storyteller uses the chair, but if they are handling a book it sure is easier.

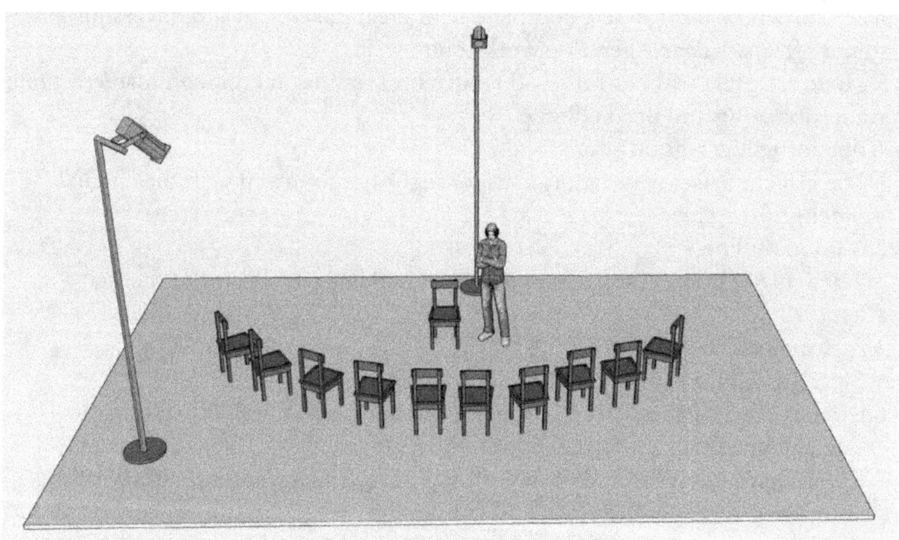

Storytelling Floor Plan

This is the exercise that really gets the adrenaline going in the classroom. The first two performances lead up to this one, and it's the last exercise that students do individually. The second half of the class is devoted to group work. You (as a teacher) should assume that your young actors will actively use what they learned from the first two exercises, and incorporate that learning for this exercise.

Step One: Choosing the monologue. I have a list of suggested monologues for this exercise, both male and female. You may vary your choices, but try to keep the monologues simple, without too much variation in age from the younger actors. Make hard copies of the monologues, put them in folders, have the students read them for about 20 minutes in each class, and let them choose one. Send electronic copies to them.

Step Two: Memorize the monologues. This is homework. Give them a week to do it, and grade them orally in class. Keep it simple by having them just say it to you, no emotion. This memory one-on-one is also an opportune time to talk about their ideas for the given circumstances of the scene, and hand them physically the Given Circumstances form, or email it to them after the meeting.

> Memorizing is hard. I memorize by rote, repeating over and over till it becomes second nature. I find that works best. I try not to put any inflection or emotion when I memorize, just as bland as I can make it. I'll add all that emotion stuff later, when I know a bit more about what I'm doing in a scene. Other actors memorize using a recording device, such as an iPhone, iPad, listening to themselves say the line over and over again. Same idea essentially – repetition. Hey, whatever works best.

Step Three: The pre-performance performance. I think this is essential. About a week and a half after this exercise starts, have the actors perform 5 lines from the monologue to get them into performance practice, and give them a feel what it's like to sweat it out on the stage. They are grateful for this portion. Very often, they have no idea of how nervous or frightened they will get till they do it. Establish good preparation: Tell them to take their time, think through the entire monologue, visualize where they are, and what they will do. Breathe to help relax. Get set, and call "curtain" to indicate they have started. This is not meant to be the final performance, so critique primarily on preparation, and the small indications of where you think they are going with the piece. Try to encourage what is working, and problem solve what is not.

<u>Step Four:</u> The final performance, about two weeks after the exercise has started. Actors hand in their given circumstances worksheet the day they perform, either by hand, or preferably as an email to you before class so that you can go over it before you see the performance. How you assess their work is on a grade sheet in the appendix. By now your class should be fairly adept at giving critique, so let them take over feedback time, but give your final say at the end, summing up what you've heard, then giving the performer a chance to explain what he was trying to do.

<u>Step Five:</u> If the work leaves much to be desired, have the student do the monologue again. Some people just take longer to learn, and need that honest feedback to help them understand that this acting stuff is hard work!

Classroom exercises leading up to the performances should focus on given circumstances improvisations and the study of the Stanislavski and Meyerhold techniques.

<u>Given Circumstances Worksheet</u>

<u>NAME</u>   **CHARACTER**

<u>WHERE</u> (Describe the location of the monologue. Be as specific as you can. Dimensions, colors, objects, furniture, and so on. If there are other people in the area, where and who are they?)

<u>WHO</u> (Describe the character you are portraying. How old? Where is s/he from? Supply a simple backstory that will help in your performance. The more specific you are, the richer the performance.)

<u>WHEN</u> (At what time does this monologue happen? Is it Winter, Spring? Is it a warm summer evening?)

<u>WHAT</u> (Are you doing something while performing the monologue? Eating breakfast, enjoying cool beverage, writing a letter? You'll find that occupying yourself will make the lines flow more naturally, and you will be less aware of the audience)

<u>WHY</u> (Write down a simple justification for why this monologue is said. Does the character have a reason for his/her anger, sadness or whatever emotion you are portraying?)

A rebellion against the declamatory artificial style used in the late 1800's.

ELEMENTS OF AN ACTION:

THE MAGIC IF - the question asked by an actor at any point of any given action is - "What would I do if I were the character in these circumstances?"

GIVEN CIRCUMSTANCES - The actor must become familiar with the environment, the time and place of the action, the conditions of life of the characters. The who, what, why, when and where of a particular situation.

IMAGINATION - The actor must learn to cultivate a mind that is rich, alert and active. He must observe people and their behavior and try to understand their mentality. He must learn to analyze, compare. He must learn to dream.

TRUTH AND BELIEF - The actor must truly believe in the make-believe world he is creating. An audience will not be deceived by an actor who is not truthful to his stage reality.

COMMUNION - The actor must put all his effort in communicating on the stage, whether verbal or not. Most importantly, the actor must find communion with his audience and become one with them. His feelings become the audience's feelings.

TEMPO-RHYTHM – Tempo refers to the internal pace of a character – how fast s/he thinks and reacts. Rhythm is the outer expression of that internal pace. Very often they are not similar. A young character may have slow tempo, but fast rhythm, and the opposite could be true for an older character.

EMOTIONAL MEMORY - The actor needs to express stage experiences and not real ones. Therefore, an actor can use an experience in his life that is analogous to the feeling needed on the stage. The stage experience becomes a "repeated" experience and not a "primary" one.

Other terms often associated with Stanislavski are SUPER-OBJECTIVE, which other theories would refer to as a theme to a play, and THROUGH LINE OF ACTION, which refers to a character's driving motivation through the duration of the play.

<u>VSEVELOD MEYERHOLD</u> (1874-1942) Appointed by Constantin Stanislavski to find an alternative approach to acting. His system has been called an opposite to that of Stanislavski. While Stanislavski seeks inner truth, Meyerhold does not. Meyerhold stresses that any emotion that occurs must be with the audience and not the actor. To Meyerhold, the director was the only creative force in the theatre. His was a dictatorial approach.

Three major concepts are associated with Meyerhold:
<u>BIOMECHANICS</u>
   Meyerhold wished each of his actors to have a body as efficient as a machine in carrying out the orders of its operator. Actors were trained in ballet, gymnastics, and circus techniques until they were able to respond instantly to the demands of the director. Meyerhold was not interested in psychological realism.
<u>THEATRICALISM</u>
   Meyerhold wished the audience to remain conscious that it was in the theatre. He removed the front curtain, had stage lights visible to the audience, used a gymnastic approach to acting, juxtaposed many contrasting dramatic elements. Meyerhold never allowed his audience to confuse theatre with real life. Theatre was an art form to him, and he felt that this art form was best used as a means for social, political and economic change - a powerful means of propaganda.
<u>CONSTRUCTIVISM</u>
   The stage, the actor and all theatrical elements were viewed by Meyerhold as a single complex machine under direct control of the director, which in this case, was him. Sets were ramps, platforms, trapezes united to make a series of heights and levels in which an actor could most efficiently work on.

<u>CONTRASTING TWO OPPOSING THEORIES OF PERFORMANCE</u>

<u>STANISLAVSKI</u>	<u>MEYERHOLD</u>
INNER FEELING	OUTER EXPRESSION
THEATRE IS TO ENTERTAIN	THEATRE IS TO EDUCATE
AUDIENCE IS TO EMPATHIZE	AUDIENCE IS INCITED TO ACTION
ACTING IS REALISTIC	ACTING IS THEATRICAL
SPECTACLE IMITATES LIFE	SPECTACLE IS THEATRICAL
<u>ACTOR</u> MUST BELIEVE IN THE REALITY OF THE STAGE EXPERIENCE	<u>AUDIENCE</u> MUST BELIEVE IN THE REALITY OF THE STAGE EXPERIENCE
EMOTION RECALL	BIOMECHANICS
ACTOR - CREATIVE FORCE	DIRECTOR - CREATIVE FORCE

II: Backstage theatre

This is essentially four parts – first, a tour of the stage and how everything backstage works. It's important for you to know this stuff yourself, so if you don't, take the time to have someone teach you.

Important terminology review:
"Heads Up!" – means something is coming down from above, in a controlled manner. It's a gentle warning.
"HEADS!" – should not be gentle. Something's falling, and it is dangerous! Get offstage as soon as possible! Offstage in this sense, is away from the overhead fly system.
The Catwalk – front of house lighting positions. If safe for students to do so, have them go up to see what they look like to the technicians who work for them.
Explain upstage, downstage, in, out, Stage Left, Center, Right.
Explain the fly system, if you have one.
Show off the shop, if you have one.
Explain dressing room etiquette, and show them dressing rooms.

Refer to the handouts as a guideline.

Second – a repeat of the acoustic demonstration. Do the acoustic exercise in the largest theatre space you have.

Third, a small lighting demonstration.

Fourth, some design exercises for fun.

Set up three lights, two in front of the actor, about 45 degrees above and to the side of the actor, and one directly in back of the actor. Have a warm colored gel (ex. Roscolux 02) and a cool gel (ex. Roscolux 51) for the front light, and a blue backlight (Roscolux 66). Have the actor get used to stage lighting. It seems a bit harsh when you first encounter it.

Simple exercises:

1) Find your light – An actor's face is not lit until he feels the light glisten on his eyebrows. It works, try it.

2.Using marks on the stage. Put an x with masking tape on the stage floor. Have the actor practice going to his mark without causing too much attention to it. Easier said than done.

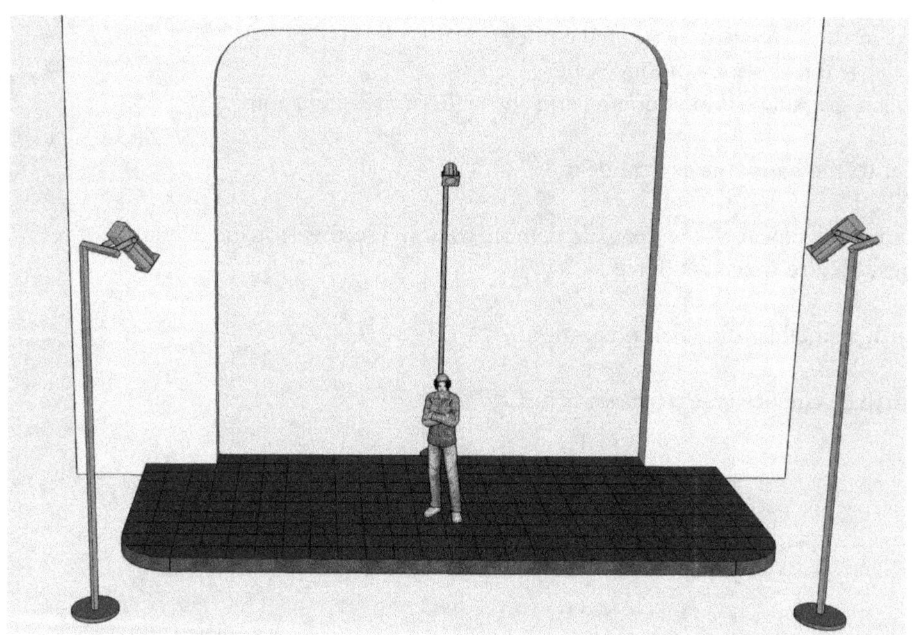

Three light Demonstration

Exercise: Design the Theme Park

Class divides into groups of three or four, depending on class size.

Group answers the following questions:

1. What are the most exciting theme parks I have been to? Why?

2. What are the current popular ideas/games for my target audience?

From your answers, formulate a design of a theme park. An example would be a theme park based on the movie Jurassic Park, or Toy Story.

Requirements of the Theme Park:

1. FOOD!
2. RIDES!
3. The standard practical things - prices of rides, food, admission.

Each member of the group should present a portion of the presentation. One to discuss overall design concept, one to discuss food, another (or two) to discuss the rides and the overall experience.

The visual presentation should be either a ground plan of the park, or a publicity poster.

The audience may be any age group. Children, Youth your age, Families, or Seniors.

Exercise: designing three dimensional emotions

Students are divided into groups of three, four or five. They are then given materials: Newspaper, scissors and masking tape. They are asked to write down a single emotion on the backside of their work and then create a three-dimensional structure (in thirty minutes at most) that best conveys the emotion.
When work is complete, there is a class presentation in which other class members first critique the work, and then group members explain how design was conceptualized.

Coaching: Students are often concerned that their interpretation of an emotion is not a universal one - this is understandable, and important to take notice of. This exercise brings out important points:
Each person has their own way of expressing emotions, and each person has their own way of receiving those same emotions.

EVALUATION: 1. The quality of the visual presentation
                   2. The quality of the oral presentation

Grade is based upon: Clarity of material,
                       Number of ideas presented,
                       Manner of presenting material to class.

Each student in the group is given a number of points for their work.

III: The Realistic Theatre Classroom Exercise

Why we do this exercise – this could be the most important exercise the class does. What is being done is a recreation of the whole process of putting on a production from the standpoint of the director-actor relationship. From choosing the play to performance, the student is given an appreciation of how the theatre machine works. The student is given tips on how to audition, how to move onstage, how stage blocking is done, how dramatic moments are created, and how a scene is essentially choreographed and conducted by the director.

Part One: a classroom discussion of how a play is chosen. You may refer to the director's portion of this book for material for this. This discussion can get rather lively. Actors get personal about shows they think are great.

Part Two: Preparation and execution of a mock audition. You've chosen a play. The scene I have used most often for this exercise is the courtroom scene from Act Three of Arthur Miller's "The Crucible." There are many interesting characters, and it is fairly balanced male and female, and strong dramatic conflict with many characters involved – a perfect teaching tool. You may pick your own.

Unfortunately, The Crucible doesn't have many lengthy monologues to use for an audition. So, I have used, for many years, the beautiful monologue Gallo says in "The Fantasticks" as my go-to audition monologue ("You wonder how these things begin…") The language is lyric, not quite modern English, which is a problem that actors encounter when working with Miller's dialogue – it's English, but just tricky enough to throw you off. There are instructions for auditioners with the audition monologue.

The audition is a cold reading, with specific instructions on how each section is performed. I advise you to invite another teacher in theatre or speech to join you in the audition section of the class - it makes it more fun and a bit more professional. Set up the classroom with a couple of desks in the back for the "casting directors," clear the stage, send each auditioner outside the classroom before each one does his stuff. Provide feedback immediately after each audition or after three auditioners.

After everyone has a chance to audition, cast the show. I like to double cast, giving more opportunity to each actor. Balance out the parts so that a lead in one cast is a smaller part in the other, and vice versa.

Part Three: Block the scene. I have a floor plan of the scene you can use, with the scene that starts with Parris' line "Now there are no spirits attacking her" and ends with Hale's dramatic exit. As you block each cast, make sure the other cast is attentive enough to write down their blocking as their other character. Review often. Blocking is very boring to cast members, mainly because it is a slow and tedious (yet necessary) process of theatre.

Part Four: Rehearse the scene. I experiment a lot as a director, and love to do it in this exercise. Here are some things you can do: play with tempo, play with emotions – such as have them do the whole scene angry, or sad, or giddy. It may seem like "play" at the time, but very often, good ideas about where these emotions would work in the scene come out of these rehearsals. Change genders – I've had great female John Proctors come out of this experiment, enough to inspire the males to be a bit more masculine.

Part Five: Perform the scene. Film it. Let the class view and critique their work. It will become very clear to actors that the camera does not lie about them not really "performing" when they think they can blend in a crowd and not be seen.

Part Six: Review the whole process. Discuss this as a class. How could they have been better? What were the things they could have done when they weren't "on" as a performer? Another reason I like the crucible scene is that only Elizabeth Proctor is offstage for most of the time. All the other characters are onstage, which helps classroom management.

Another reason I like "The Crucible" is that it brings up very important historical discussions. The trail and hanging of 19 people in Salem, Massachusetts is a sad part of American history, and the parallel 1950s McCarthy "witch hunts" in Congress lead to interesting discussion. Most students cannot fathom the situation, nor comprehend how cruel this all really was. A strong discussion often comes from why the girls had their religious "fits," writhing on the floor. Just don't let the discussion get too out of hand, as I have. It's very interesting stuff!

by Tom Jones and Harvey Schmidt

Part One

<u>GALLO</u>:   You wonder how these things begin.

Well, this begins with a glen.

It begins with a Season, which,
For want of a better word,
We might as well call September.

It begins with a forest where the woodchucks woo
And leaves wax green,
And vines entwine like lovers;

Try to see it:
Not with your eyes, for they are wise;
But with your ears:
The cool green breathing of the leaves.
And hear it with the inside of your hand:
The soundless sound of shadows flicking light.

- -

Part Two
Celebrate sensation.

Recall that secret place;
You've been there, you remember:
That special place where once -
Just once - in your crowded sunlit lifetime,
You hid away in shadows from the tyranny of time.
That spot beside the clover
Where someone's hand held your hand,
And love was sweeter than the berries,
Or the honey,
Or the stinging taste of mint.

It is September,
Before a rainfall -

A perfect time to be in love.

Instructions for auditioners: Perform this monologue as two different characters: First, as a young, naïve person who has much to learn about life – the world still needs to be explored, life is exciting! Perform the other part as an older wiser person who has been there, done that. The world is not exciting - even dark, cynical. Contrast the two parts (vocally, physically) as best you can.

<u>AUDITION INFORMATION SHEET</u> (to be handed to the teacher)

(A sample template)

NAME: GRADE:

HEIGHT:

VOCAL RANGE:

ROLE YOU'D ESPECIALLY LIKE TO PLAY:

(Notes for the teacher – these are good assessment categories for auditioning)
Strength   Articulation   Versatility   Expression

Strength – vocal and physical. Are they "big" enough for the performance space they are in? For the performance space they will perform in?

Articulation – English is all about the consonants! Listen for terminal consonant sound.

Versatility – Was there a difference in the first and second reading?

Expression – How lyrical was the reading of the monologue? Did the actor "color" words well?

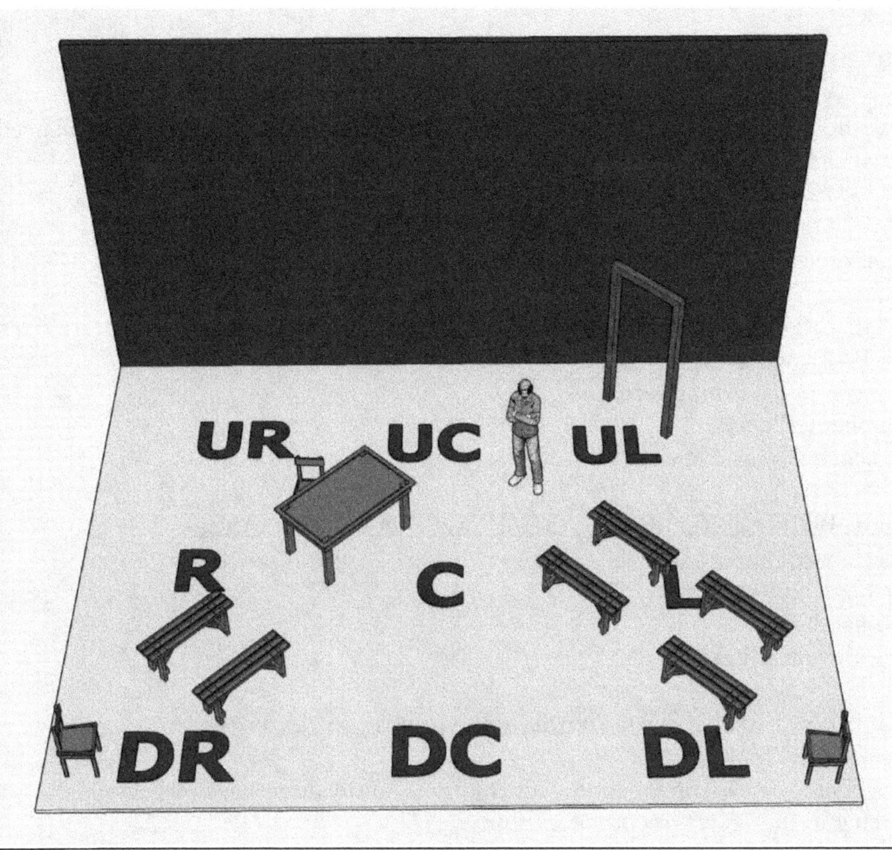

<u>Stage Blocking</u> - The positioning of actors by a director.
The most powerful and prominent stage area is <u>down center</u>. <u>Downstage</u> means toward the audience; <u>Upstage</u> means away from the audience. <u>Stage right</u> means an actor's right as he faces the audience. <u>Stage left</u>, the actor's left facing the audience. The word "<u>cross</u>" (abbreviated "X") means to move from one area to another. Thus "cross down right" would be written XDR in stage shorthand.

<u>Stage Business</u> - the movement (in character) of an actor once positioned by a director. This usually refers to mannerisms, gesture, facial expression. The actor needs to "<u>open</u>" or "<u>cheat</u>" his/her body to the audience as much as possible, to assure that the audience sees what it should onstage. This usually means a three-quarter turn of the body to the audience and a profile of the face to the fellow actor.

The Six Rehearsal Phases

A two-hour main stage play needs at least six weeks of rehearsal. A musical will need at least eight weeks.
ROUGH EQUATION:
One minute of performance = two hours of rehearsal
Six rehearsal weeks for a play:

1. THE INTRODUCTORY PHASE – first day
First Play reading
Character notes from director
Preliminary Blocking
Play schedules/deadlines

2. THE BLOCKING/BUSINESS/MEMORIZATION PHASE – a week, week and a half
Blocking, movement notes
Prop handling
Final memorization

3. THE EXPERIMENTAL PHASE – two to three weeks
"Breaking the mold"
Actor/Director experimentation with emotions, motivation, stage business
Working to the "guts" or core of a scene.

4. THE POLISHING PHASE – a week
Cleaning up - making choices, what works, what doesn't
Polishing the rough edges of a Performance, special rehearsals
Run-throughs

5. THE TECHNICAL PHASE – a week
Actors/Director/Technicians adjust to one another.
Tech rehearsals, Costumes

6. THE PERFORMANCE PHASE - three days
High-energy rehearsals without the audience, or a preview group.
Run-throughs with all aspects of theatre working in full gear.

FINALLY, OPENING NIGHT!

This is where the class gets to show off what it knows (and doesn't know) about putting on a show. The scenes are two or three characters depending on class size, and students are responsible for the properties and costumes that they need for the scene. They rehearse and block the scene by themselves. What is provided for them are the set properties (tables, doors and chairs) and simple lighting (but the lighting is optional)

Part One: Final groups and their scenes are assigned. You will get a feel, through the semester, what actors work well with others, and pair up those who do. I am particularly fond of the book **Rash Acts** by Conrad Bishop and Elizabeth Fuller, and have used their satirical pieces with great characters and dialogue for years. The best pieces (and these are personal choices, there are more in the book) are Happy Anniversary (one male, one female) Tell It Like It Is (one male, one female) Dalmatian (two females) and Doors (one male, one female, though 2 females is pretty interesting, too) Watchers (two males, one female) Floor plans for the scenes are provided.

Part Two: Classroom rehearsal, with stage props set up. Give each group 20 minutes for actual stage time during class hours. Observe rehearsal habits – there often is a lot of playing going on, and that's ok up to a point (the class can be fun after all) but it's your job to keep them focused.

> A word to the wise: Start using props as soon as possible! Most of the mistakes that happen in performance come from prop malfunctions. I have too many stories about this, from gun misfires to a song about a "Strong Bridge" that collapsed as the song was sung.

Part Three: Pre-performance performance. Just the same as the monologue section of the class, except now they are working as a team. It's especially good for them to practice entering into the scene, what happens before an entrance, action before lines start. Have costumes and props used during this rehearsal.

> A very important theatre word comes out of this type of rehearsal – recovery. An actor must cope with the inevitable fluffed line, dropped prop, costume malfunction. Actors may not stop during this rehearsal – deal with the issue, be it an improvised line, or just simply fixing things as you would in real life, while you say the line. The more recovery is practiced, the more confident an actor gets about making mistakes on the stage, and they do happen often!

Part Four: – the Final performance. Remind the class about the order of performance. Do this the class day before this happens. The scenes should be watched by all - no cramming of line rehearsals and so on by other groups. Teach appropriate crowd behavior.

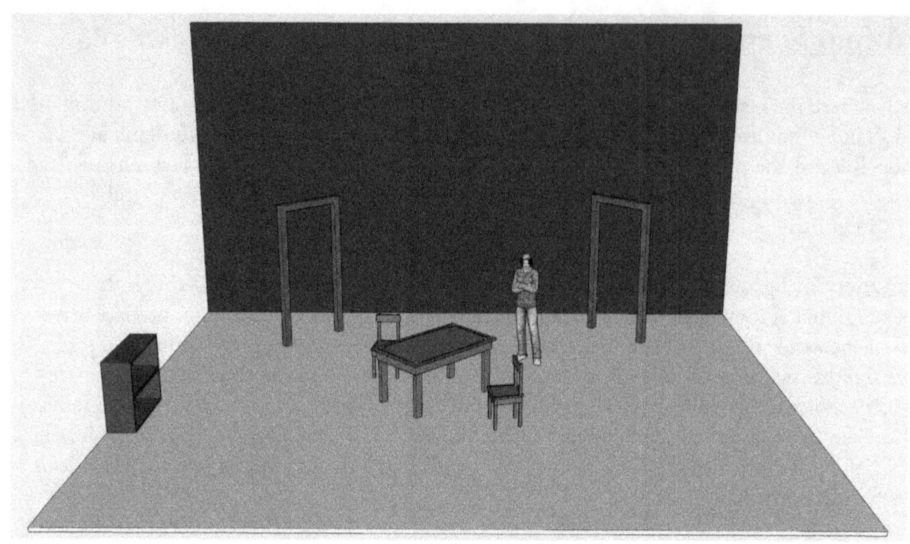

Floor plan for Dalmation, Tell it like is, Anniversary, Watchers

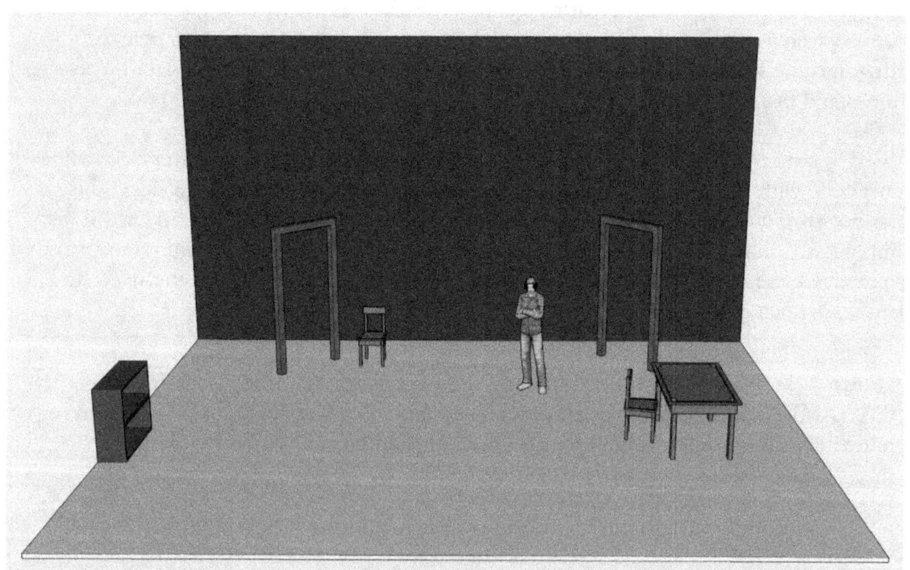

Doors floor plan

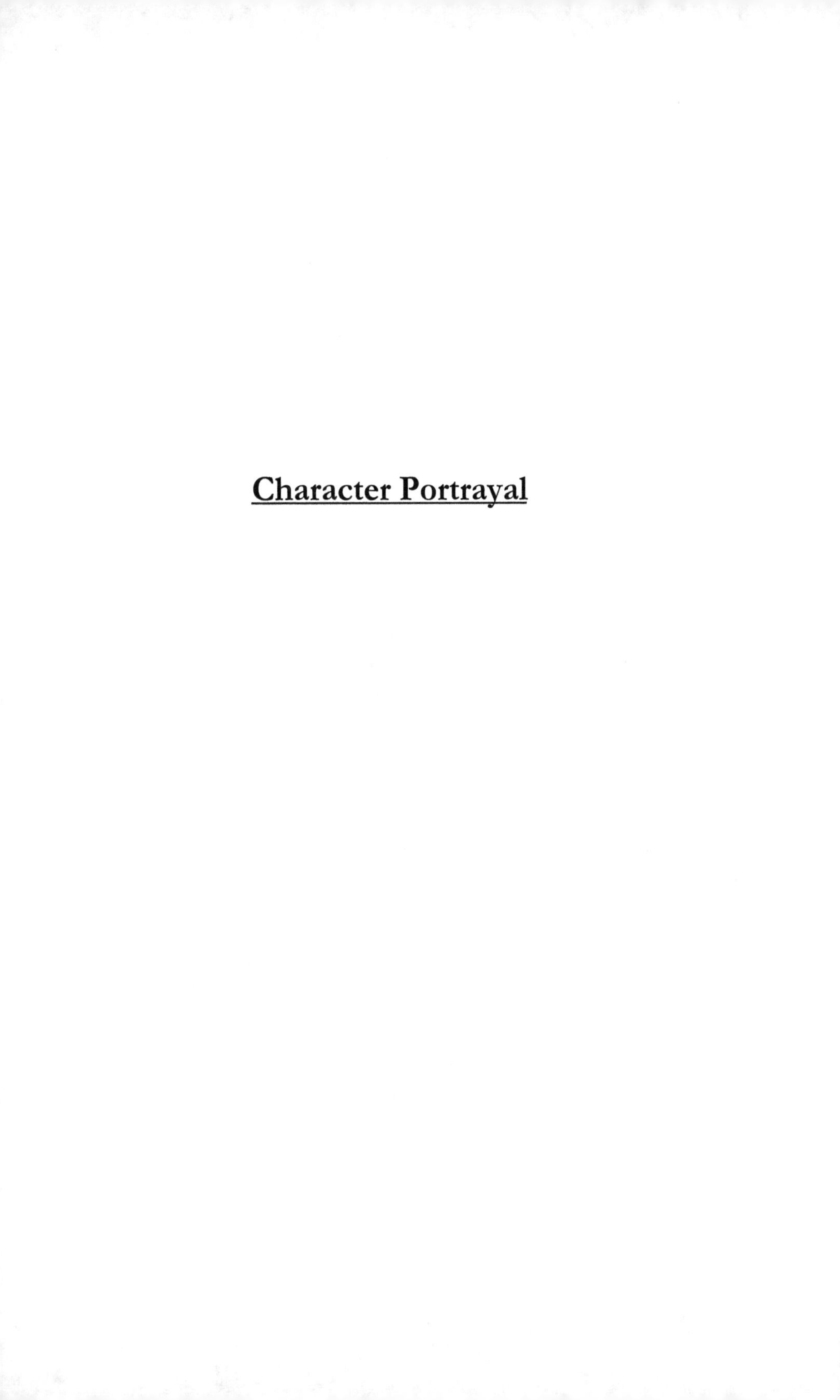

Character Portrayal

The format for the entire semester of this class revolves around four main performance exercises: Two are monologues, and two are two-person (possibly three-person) scenes. The first two exercises last until midterm time, and the last two the second half of class. I like to think of the final scene as a performance final exam. Classroom training exercises in each section are focused towards that particular performance exercise.

The first monologue is called the Voice/Attitude monologue. The focus of the actor's work is on what the voice can do to create a strong and believable character. It was first called the "accent" monologue, as I wanted students to learn accents to help characterization. While some actors were successful with this exercise, others were not. I had assumed that mimicking accents was pretty easy – I guess it isn't. I once thought I had my British accent down, and was told more often than not it was terrible. Others thought it was fine – it's a pretty subjective thing.
The change in focus was necessary. I like the actor to try the accent, or better yet the "attitude" created by the accent. Evaluation is not on accent perfection, but on what the accent does to help create a character.
For those who can't do the accent thing, despite trying very hard, I ask them to choose an "attitude" for the character – which can be translated as working on a voice that is very different from their own, such as performing an older voice. It still involves a lot of work, trust me. It is very hard for a young performer to "unlearn" his speech patterns, and this exercise does that.
This new approach has been much more successful.

The second monologue is called the Veil/Persona monologue. The focus of this exercise is on bodywork and hopefully, body transformation to create character. I like the word "Veil" – it's a term coined by Michael Chekhov, and it says it pretty well. I use Persona (which means "the mask worn by an actor"), but what they both imply is that the actor creates a new body that performs this monologue. What is also implied in this exercise is that the work done in the first exercise carries over – we don't all of a sudden abandon the voice work. Added on to this are more requirements, such as good application of props and costume. This is the last time I work with an actor individually with their rehearsal and performance technique, and I like to evaluate everything, to the point of being super picky. I try to spend as much time outside of class with actors for this, as the classroom can be hectic and impersonal. The critique from other class members should be specific also – leave nothing overlooked, if possible.

<u>The third exercise is an intense two-person scene that tries to explore the excitement of working with another actor.</u> The class training exercises are especially important for this. They are difficult to do, and yet quite simple to explain. I have found the play "The Shadowbox" by Michael Cristofer an excellent teaching play for this. Great characters, great issues, very dramatic, and, like "The Crucible, " great classroom discussions. Language is strong (R or MA, as TV-15 would say) in this play, so you may want to tame it some.

<u>The final scene should be a celebration of everything good about two-person scene work.</u> I have used two different plays for this, and you can take your pick. Both are difficult, for different reasons. "Home Free" by Lanford Wilson is two-character play that is powerful, but deals with incest, and is disturbing for some actors. However, it is a great teaching play about subtext and character. The second is "August: Osage County," by Tracy Letts - again, a complicated play with powerful characters and mature situations and language. Students love to perform this play, and it isn't just about being able to swear onstage. It didn't get the Pulitzer (as did "The Shadowbox") for nothing.

<table><tr><td>

About swearing. It comes up all the time. Yes or no? I have changed over the years. I use to cut out every swear word in every scene. I once performed the part of Lee in "True West, " made him such a vile guy that the director wasn't aware I took out all the swear words – Lee was a true scumbag. But there are plays where you just can't do that – the play just doesn't work without the swearing. If you are touchy about this, I would suggest using "A Streetcar Named Desire" for your final scene. How ironic, I'm suggesting a play with no swearing, but it implies sexual assault. Oh boy.

</td></tr></table>

Exercises to start the class going

THE NEUTRAL SPACE CONCEPT

One of the most important problems an actor faces is his fear of the performance space. Many performers have no problem acting in hallways, their living rooms, bathrooms. However, once any one of these spaces are redefined as a "stage" or a performance space, the actor freezes up. Fear of the performance space is often called stage fright, and it can manifest itself in many different ways: "butterflies" in the stomach, sweaty palms, rapid heartbeat, nausea. It is important for the actor to view the performance space as a non-threatening environment.

The neutral space concept tries to deal directly with this problem. It is a form of visualization that makes the actor view the stage as a comfort zone, a place that the actor will actually find release and good feelings.

THE NEUTRAL SPACE VISUALIZATION EXERCISE

Have all players (actors) lie down on their backs, stretched out comfortably on the performance space floor. You may have soft music playing, or better yet "white noise" - such as the sound of waves or a quiet breeze. Bring the lights down in the room. Read the paragraph below as calmly and clearly as you can. Or better yet, use this as a guide – make one up of your own.

"I want you to relax. Not by falling asleep, but by closing your eyes and imagining that parts of your body are getting very heavy. imagine your feet getting heavy. Your calves. Your knees. Imagine your waist getting so heavy that it feels like it is melting into the floor. Imagine your chest getting heavy. Your neck. Your head.

Take deep breaths. Feel the breaths coming in through the use of your diaphragm. Keep your eyes moving around even if they are closed. You are still active, but now it is your mind that is light, as your body is heavy. Visualize a blue dot in that black void in front of you. You are that blue dot, and you are going to leave behind your heavy body and go on a mental trip with me.

All around you is blue as you rise above your body, leaving this dark room behind, and now you are flying in the sky, and all around you is a wonderful deep blue, as you are way above the earth above the clouds, totally free.

Enjoy this space for a while. Take some dives below. You are like a bird, light and free.

Way down below you see a small island in the deep blue ocean. You dive down to see this island, and you realize that nobody lives there. A small beautiful island in the middle of the ocean, and this is your island. Your space that you can roam around and expire and nobody will tell you where you can and cannot go because it is yours and you are totally free. You can swim, you can fly, you can walk, you can sing, scream, cry, laugh, and not worry about what others may think because there are no others. It belongs to you - it is your space.

Explore this space. Find out all you can about it. Visualize it, create it, make it truly your own creation. It is a place of release, of rest, of comfort - it is home for your mind. It is a home of peace, of tranquility, of joy. It is your heaven.

Remember your feelings. You will need to recall those feelings later on. You will be back, because it is a place you've found, you've created, and you will always remember.

Pull yourself away for now, be that bird that flies high up to that big blue sky above, soaring, swooping, floating. Fly back to this room, slowly. Fly back into your mind that is in your body.

Rediscover your body. Visualize that light feeling you had as a bird and bring that lightness back to your head, neck, arms, chest, waist, legs and feet, slowly and in that order. Slowly pull yourselves to a sitting position."

<u>FOLLOW UP</u>

Spend some time talking with players about their feelings in the neutral space that they have created. This space is a comfort zone, an area they can mentally go to before they perform to relax them. A second transition can be to have players visualize that those comfortable feelings can be transferred to the stage, if they visualize that the stage itself is their neutral space.

Early on in an advanced class like this, spend time going over these acting/movement/prop exercises. You assume that the actors know this, but go over it anyway. You'd be surprised how much of this slips through the cracks in instruction.

Movement across the stage. Down, Up, Right, Left. Have the players close their eyes when they do this.

Discuss and demonstrate on and off stage.

Stage areas.

Blocking using a clock as reference – such as, stand at 11 o'clock – I use this for theatre in the round.

The handling of drinks, whatever they are. Hard liquor, Mixed drink, Beer, Wine, Coffee, Tea (hot or cold) Juice. Use real cups and water. Not pantomime.

Hugs. Most stage hugs are pathetic. Hey, full body hugs if you please!! None of this tentative, top half body hug thing. Totally unbelievable.

Kisses. First thing – breath mints!! Keep it professional.

Handshakes. Never the wet noodle handshake, ever! Firm! Confident! Strong!

Stage positions, "opening" to the audience. Illustrate differences of two and three people on the stage.

"upstaging"

And at the end, advise actors to bring their own props to rehearsal. Doesn't have to be the real thing, just something about the same weight and size. No invisible prop stuff.

Exercises for
The Attitude/Voice Monologue

The Neutral Voice Concept – a process to expand vocal range.

To understand this concept, it is first necessary to go through the steps in producing sound through the human voice mechanism. The brain registers thought, calls upon the nerves that cause the lungs to fill up with air, supplying the force that causes the vocal chords to vibrate, of which particular base tones and harmonics are reinforced in the cavities in the head. These tones are then further defined by the facial "mask" (with such parts as the teeth, the tongue, the palate, the glottis) into audible forms of communication. Through time the body develops a particular "style" in speech due to the repetition and reinforcement of particular speech patterns. This may be in the form of an accent, a lisp, a slur, mumbling, over articulation. It is important to note that mannerisms and speech patterns are an acquired personal and social thing.

To effectively increase vocal flexibility and range, it becomes important to the actor to develop a second "voice" for the stage - a voice with a wider pitch range, a voice without accents or mannerisms, a voice of power. This is the NEUTRAL VOICE.

The NEUTRAL VOICE for the stage must have these basic requirements:

1. Strength - through the development of good breathing technique, frugal use of breath.
2. Articulation - through the development of proper articulation and speed in the speech process.
3. Versatility - though the continual work in increasing the vocal range with exercises in pitch and resonance control.
4. Expression - through exercises that emphasize the use of all the elements above in producing sound that best express words, phrases, and thoughts.

EXTENDING THE NEUTRAL VOICE RANGE

1. Imagine your voice as a musical instrument. The lowest note that you can sing (this is the low voice that you wake up with in the morning) is DO. This is your LOW TONE. Sing up to FA. This is your CENTER TONE. Then sing up to the upper DO. This is your HIGH TONE. At this point, this will be your "range" as a voice. Experiment to see if this is a range different from your normal speaking voice. If it isn't that is quite all right. You are speaking in your best range. Most people speak in a higher range than they need to.

Original Neutral Range

				D	R	M	F	S	L	T	D				
				O	E	I	A	O	A	I	O				

2. Work to develop strength in this range, for it may be the range that you use the most. Most people will gravitate to their normal speaking range when they perform characters, and that is because they are most comfortable in that speaking range. The more you practice the neutral range, the more comfortable you will be with it. In the long run, it does you the most good to make the neutral voice your normal one. After all, you do want a voice with power, flexibility, expression, and clarity, don't you?

3. Work to develop pitch range. Expand the higher and lower ranges, keeping your CENTER TONE at the same place. Work so that these new pitches have the same power as the "older" ones.

Expanded Range

F	S	L	T	D	R	M	F	S	L	T	D	R	M	F	S
A	O	A	I	O	E	I	A	O	A	I	O	E	I	A	O

4. Once you have expanded your range to, say, two octaves, move your CENTER TONE around. Two examples are diagrammed below: The original low-center-high tones are bold.

Expanded Neutral Range with Lower Center Tone

F	S	L	T	**D**	R	M	**F**	S	L	T	**D**	R	M	F	S
A	O	A	I	**O**	E	I	**A**	O	A	I	**O**	E	I	A	O

Expanded Neutral Range with Higher Center Tone

F	S	L	T	**D**	R	M	**F**	S	L	T	**D**	R	M	F	S
A	O	A	I	**O**	E	I	**A**	O	A	I	**O**	E	I	A	O

From this diagram, you can see the process by which variety in vocal characterization is first achieved by developing a new vocal range for a specific character the actor wishes to portray. The actor may want to use the first range for a more authoritative, middle-aged role. The second range may be perfect for a youthful, insecure role.

Developing the new range is the springboard for many other vocal techniques the actor can apply to the new character voice.

What makes this technique all the more powerful is that the character is much less likely to be affected by the mannerisms of the actor himself, thus creating a very effective new stage persona.

Note that a new process for formulating words occurs when the neutral sound concept is in effect: The brain now calls for a sound to be produced, but the body, now trained, goes through a new mechanical process that best uses the resonances, speech patterns, affectations necessary for each particular role to be performed.

Discovering your Character's Instrument.

Imagine that you are in an orchestra. Before you sit down to play the piece, you need to find your instrument in the orchestra – are you a violin, cello, horn? So it is with a character in a play. Find the instrument of that character, and establish a sound for it. What is the range of that instrument? What does that instrument sound like loud or soft? What are its tonal qualities?

Character Placement -

Here is a simple placement template

Tempo	Volume	Pitch	Tone
Slow	Soft	Low	Mellow
Medium	Medium	Middle	Regular
Fast	Loud	High	Harsh

This is taking the neutral voice concept (NVC) to another level. NVC does not take the other qualities of sound (besides pitch) into consideration. Consider this NVC on steroids.

As an introductory exercise:
Plot the template (in your voice) for each of the seven ages (in As You Like It) described in Jacques monologue "All the World's the Stage". How would **you** sound in each one? Jacques is describing the seven ages of man, and it is appropriate to play each part in the voice that each age would sound like.

JACQUES: All the world's a stage,
And all the men and women merely players:
They have their exits and their entrances;
And one man in his time plays many parts,
His acts being seven ages.

At first the infant,
Mewling and puking in the nurse's arms.

And then the whining schoolboy, with his satchel
And shining morning face, creeping like snail
Unwillingly to school.

And then the lover,
Sighing like furnace, with a woeful ballad
Made to his mistress' eyebrow.

Then a soldier,
Full of strange oaths and bearded like a pard
Jealous in his honour, sudden and quick in quarrel,
Seeking the bubble reputation
Even in the cannon's mouth.

And then the justice,
In fair round belly with good capon lined
With eyes severe and beard of formal cut,
Full of wise saws and modern instances
And so he plays his part.

The sixth age shifts
Into the lean and slipper'd pantaloon,
With spectacle on nose and pouch on side,
His youthful hose, well saved, a world too wide
For his shrunk shank; and his big manly voice,
Turning again toward childish treble, pipes
And whistles in his sound.

Last scene of all,
That ends this strange eventful history,
Is second childishness and mere oblivion,
Sans teeth, sans eyes, sans taste, sans every thing.

Word Coloring – a process to help the actor express his emotions in the words he says. To illustrate how the system works, consider these lines taken from a Welsh poem:

Deep peace of the running wave to you
Deep peace of the shining stars to you
Deep peace of Christ, the light of the world, to you.

Step One: Break the poem down into segments. First, line, then phrase, then word. The poem has three lines…
Line one - Deep peace of the running wave to you
Line one has three phrases - Deep peace/of the running wave/to you
The First phrase, two words – Deep/peace
For longer poems, add *stanza* to the list of elements for division. For plays with long monologues, *paragraphs* would be added. We have the word *deep* to color.

Step Two: Ask yourself these questions:
1) What does the word mean?
2) How does it affect me?
3) What are the consonant and vowel sounds of the word?
4) What sounds can I use to help me convey the way it affects me?
Deep means "placed far down" or "solemn, grave." The word affects me in a somber way. It tends to make me feel low, sadder heavier in thoughts. The consonant and vowel sounds are (d) (ē) (p). The vowel sound (ē) can best help express this feeling because I can extend it to make the word seem slower and more profound. However, this is not the only way a word can be colored.

The four elements of word coloring are duration (slow-fast), volume (soft-loud), pitch (low-high) and tone (smooth-harsh Word coloring need not be done on every word in a poem or play. However, with more words colored, word meaning is better expressed, and more importantly, the actor expresses himself better. The vowel need not be the only sound within the word used to "color." In the word *peace*, for example, the extended terminal (s) sound would best relay the feeling of tranquility the word gives.

<u>Step Three</u>: Move up to the phrase. What word within the phrase is more important? What word should I color more? I choose *peace* to emphasize more, as *deep* just describes *peace*. And we add another element for coloring: the use of pause. When pause is used within phrases, it puts emphasis on the next word; within lines and paragraphs it suggests change of thought.
Step Four: Move up to the line. What phrases are more important, and thus emphasized more vocally? All elements of coloring may be used. You may choose to write out the line as follows:

<u>Deep</u> /**peace**// of the <u>running</u> **wave**/ to **you**.

<u>Underlining</u> indicates coloring, but not as much as words that have been made **bold**. The bar indicate pause, double bars even longer pause. You may choose your own way to mark up a script or poem to indicate words to color.
Step Five: Work on the entire poem. Here are my choices for word coloring:

<u>Deep</u> /**peace**// of the <u>running</u> **wave**/ to **you**.
<u>Deep</u> /**peace**// of the <u>shining</u> **stars**/ to **you**.
<u>Deep</u> /**peace**// of **Christ**// the <u>light</u> of the **world** /to **you**.

<u>One final note</u>: Notice that I have not chosen at this particular point to write down how I color the word, just that I feel that it should be colored. You will find that over time, you will change how you color words and possibly even the words you color through the process called rehearsal.

An Exercise in Word Coloring

Sonnet 91
William Shakespeare

Some glory in their birth, some in their skill,
Some in their wealth, some in their bodies' force,
Some in their garments, though new-fangled ill,
Some in their hawks and hounds, some in their horse;

And every humour hath his adjunct pleasure,
Wherein it finds a joy above the rest:
But these particulars are not my measure;
All these I better in one general best.

Thy love is better than high birth to me,
Richer than wealth, prouder than garments' cost,
Of more delight than hawks or horses be;
And having thee, of all men's pride I boast:

>Wretched in this alone, that thou mayst take
>All this away and me most wretched make.

Some hints for performance:

This sonnet is divided into 4 parts:
1st four lines ABAB
2nd four lines CDCD
3rd four lines EFEF
4th quatrain GG

A general format for many sonnets is that the first eight lines are describing a situation, and then the 9th line has an "answer" or a resolution to the first eight lines. There are times when the resolution is in the last two lines.

The end of lines does not necessarily mean the end of ideas. They can wrap around to the next line.

It's a good idea to memorize Shakespeare in a neutral voice. That way you do not get into a singsong pattern that is often common with iambic pentameter (stressed/unstressed speech patterns).

Paraphrase the sonnet. Understand what the words mean. Then convey that understanding in your performance. The technical tools you have to work with are variations in:
Tempo – fast slow
Pitch – high low
Tone – harsh smooth
Volume – loud soft

Mark your sonnet up with your own "performance shorthand". Use single bars as short pauses, double as longer pauses. Circle words you "color".
Write the words as if notes on a musical staff – whatever works best for you!

AMADEUS
by Peter Shaffer

Antonio Salieri, court composer to Joseph of Austria (in his mid thirties), describes the first time he hears Mozart's music.

SALIERI: And then right away the music began. I heard it through the door – some Serenade. At first only vaguely – too horrified to attend. But presently, the sound insisted – a solemn Adagio in E flat.

It started simply enough – just a pulse in the lowest registers – bassoons and bassett horns – like a rusty squeeze box. It would have been comic except for the slowness, which gave it instead a kind of serenity.

And then, suddenly, high above it, sounded a single note on the oboe. It hung there, unwavering, piercing me through – till breath could hold it no longer, and then a clarinet withdrew it out of me, and sweetened it into a phrase of such delight it had me trembling.

The squeezebox groaned louder, and over it the higher instruments wailed and warbled, throwing lines of sound around me – long lines of pain around and through me.

I called up to my sharp old God – "What is this? What?"

But the squeezebox went on and on, and the pain cut deeper and deeper into my shaking head, until suddenly I was running, dashing through the side-door, stumbling downstairs into the street, into the cold night, gasping for life.

"What? What is this? Tell me Signore! What is this pain? What is this need in the sound? Forever unfulfillable, yet fulfilling him who hears it, utterly. Is it your need? Can it be yours?

(pause)

Dimly the music sounded from the salon above. Dimly the stars shown on the empty street.

I was suddenly terrified.

It seemed to me that I had heard a voice of God –
And it was the voice of an obscene child!

Sample annotated monologue

A review of the voice process: These notes are a synthesis of my notes in my journal of Amadeus.

This was perhaps the most difficult monolog to memorize in the whole play. I memorized this for the audition, and even with that, when it came to memorizing it for the play, the additional pressure was that the words came with music.

I was reacting to a piece of music that Peter Shaffer had picked, that was the inspiration for the monolog. It was when I heard the music that I really got turned on to it.

While technically difficult, (try sounding natural and emotional and spontaneous when you have to time it PERFECTLY to music!) it was always (along with the final monologue of act one) the most beautiful monolog in the play to do, and there wasn't one night that I didn't hear a sob in the audience from someone who understood Salieri's pain.

That was the difficulty of the piece. I felt as a performer, that this was my only chance to finally "get the audience on my side" in the whole play. Yeah, he was evil, but in the long run, he was "the good guy." And the monologue explains why everything was so unfair!

Tempo was difficult. I couldn't really control it too much, as the tempos of the performance dictated when that great line about the oboe solo had to come when we heard the oboe's first note.

But within that tight framework, I played with pitch a lot. Must have been 20 minutes each day working on this particular monologue, very technically.

I understood the emotions from the context of the play, and used two emotional "keys" of anger and sadness when I needed to. The amazing thing is that I really didn't need to use the keys much. I got him. I've been jealous of other people's talent, not to his extent, but I could certainly use that feeling I had and amplify it – and I did that technically.

I used emotion recall for the moment of hearing the oboe. I'm a fan of Ralph Vaughn Williams, and when "Fantasia on a theme by Thomas Tallis" wouldn't work some nights, a split second later I would recall the climactic moment in Samuel Barber's Adagio for Strings.

It wasn't until halfway through the rehearsals that I finally found Mozart's music beautiful on its own. Then emotion recall wasn't needed..

<u>**FEMALE**</u>

1.<u>For Colored Girls Who Have Considered Suicide When The Rainbow Is Enuf</u> By Ntozake Shange
begins... **<u>CRYSTAL</u>** the next day beau willie...
ends...and he dropped em

1.<u>Making Noise Quietly</u> By Robert Holman
begins... **<u>HELENE</u>**: He was a soldier...
ends ...When I was better he had my head shaved again.

<u>The Miracle Worker</u> By William Gibson
begins... **<u>ANNIE:</u>** The Asylum...
ends...She's strong enough.

<u>Old Flames</u> By Ted Whitehead
begins.... **<u>MURIEL</u>**: He was heavy with...
ends...Don't you let yourself be cheated, like I was.

<u>Richard III</u> Act I Scene III, lines 196-233 (edited) By Shakespeare
begins... **<u>MARGARET</u>**: Give way, dull clouds...
ends...thou detested Richard!

1.<u>Stand And Deliver</u> By Robert Bella
begins... **<u>RAFAELA</u>**: Dear Mama.
ends...Con todo mi amor y que Dios te bendiga.

1.<u>Summertree</u> By Ron Cowen
begins... **<u>MOTHER</u>**: You know, when it comes,
ends...even know if I was crying for Ginger...or my son.

1.<u>Talking With</u> By Jane Martin
begins...**<u>ANNA MAE:</u>** If I had one wish in my life,
ends...It's our dreams make us what we are.

1. By Larry Shue
begins...**<u>CATHERINE</u>**: Mind if I sit down here?
ends...You're a good listener. You are.

<u>MALE</u>

1) **<u>Bingo</u>** By Edward Bond
begins...**<u>SHAKESPEARE:</u>**   I went to the river yesterday.
ends...Still perfect. Still beautiful.

2) **<u>All I Really Needed To Know I Learned In Kindergarten</u>**
By Robert Fulghum
begins...**<u>ED:</u>** This is kind of personal.
ends...I'm absolutely certain of it.

3) **<u>Endgame</u>** By. Samuel Beckett
begins...**<u>HAMM</u>**: One day, you'll be blind, like me.
ends...there won't be anyone left to have pity on.

4) **<u>Equus</u>** By Peter Shaffer
begins...**<u>DYSART</u>**: *All right!*   He'll be delivered from madness.
ends...And it never comes out.

5) **<u>The Laramie Project</u>** By Moises Kauffman
begins...**<u>RULAN STACEY:</u>** At twelve midnight on Monday,
ends...from the moment he got there.

6) **<u>Slingblade</u>** By Billy Bob Thornton
begins...**<u>KARL</u>**: I reckon what you'd wantin' to know is what I'ma doin' in here.
ends...I don't reckon I got no reason to kill nobody again. Mm.

7) **<u>Amadeus</u>** By Peter Shaffer
begins...**<u>SALIERI:</u>** And then, right away, the music began.
ends...And it was the voice of an obscene child!

8) **<u>Man Of La Mancha</u>** By Dale Wasserman
begins...**<u>CERVANTES:</u>** My friend, I have lived almost fifty years,
ends...and not as it ought to be!

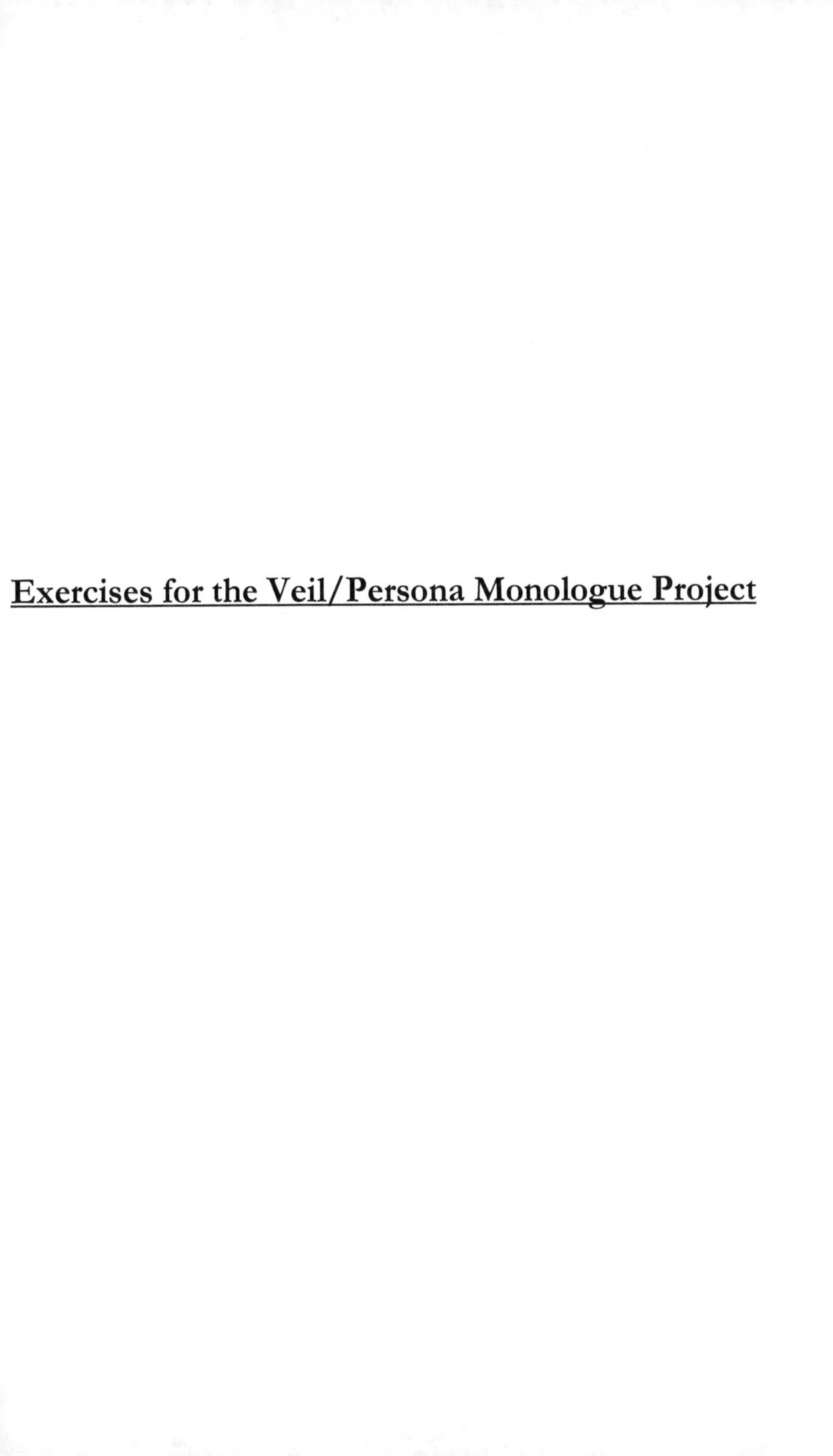

Exercises for the Veil/Persona Monologue Project

The Neutral Body Concept

This technique assumes that the actor and his character physically have some common ground: that is the good posture you were both born with. Both of you, later in life, were affected by society and personal history - enough to change your posture, face, mannerisms, how you dress and so on.

The actor must rid himself of these "acquired" stances, gestures, attitudes, mannerisms and go back physically to the common ground with the character, which is termed the NEUTRAL BODY. The Neutral body is not "held" - there is no tension- especially in the arms, legs and face.

Steps to aligning your body to be "neutral":

1. Stand with legs shoulder width apart, toes forward. Have a full-length mirror at your side, or if not possible, have a fellow actor observe you. Is your posture straight? Focus on the center of your body, the pelvic area. Is it thrust backward (swayback) or forward (pelvic thrust)? If so, shift your weight to the heels of your feet. Twist your pelvis on its axis by using your hands at your sides to turn the pelvis. Keep your back straight. This should correct the problem. It may feel awkward at first, and may take some time getting used to. You are "unlearning" years of posture dictated by society and peers.

2. Straighten your shoulders by rotating your arms backwards and then dropping them to your sides. This eliminates droopy shoulders.

3. Straighten your head by dropping your head back, and then forward, keeping your neck in place. This works much better with your actor friend gently holding your neck as you do so. You will feel a wonderful stretch.

4. Neutralize your face by dropping the jaws as far as possible, opening your mouth wide, then returning it to a position wherein your jaw is slightly open but your lips are shut. The eyes are wide open, alert, but eyebrows and forehead are relaxed. You may need someone to massage upper facial muscles, as they may be naturally tense.

5. Evaluate the whole picture, using this checklist:
a) Posture straight, without tension.
b) Shoulders comfortably rested in the middle of the chest area (again, no tension)
c) Face neutral in expression.

Practice getting your body into the neutral position without thought, so that it is automatic.

<u>Step One:</u> Turn to the first page of your script and find out whom the author is. Research the author. Popular dramatists, notably Tennessee Williams and Eugene O'Neill write about themselves – if not directly autobiographical, at least some situations in their plays are taken out of their own history. Where an author lived often influences a play. A big example of that is Tennessee Williams' "A Streetcar Named Desire, " taken directly out of a period in his life where he lived in New Orleans. Authors sometimes write plays that describe or a part of a historical or artistic period. Shakespeare wrote in the Renaissance earlier in his life, and his later plays are Mannerist. These styles are quite different, and they influence the tone of his plays. Authors often show personal political and social attitudes. Garcia-Lorca had deep feelings about the social mores of Spain and brought these feelings into "Blood Wedding" and "The House of Bernardo Alba." Gather as much data as possible, find pictures of the author and his family; seemingly trivial facts may later provide strong clues to character visualization.

<u>Step Two:</u> Script research and Analysis. Read the play three times for three different reasons.
1) Read as if you are an audience member, seeing the play for the first time. How did reading the play affect you? Was action evident in words or stage directions, or did you have to imagine a lot? Was there a particular tone to the play – a dark comedy, a frivolous musical, a humorous tragedy (there are such things!)? If you are not impressed you can either opt out of auditioning for this play or talk to the director about it – maybe there was something you didn't catch about the show that he will be able to explain.

2) Read the play for character data gathering. The author often gives a brief description of every character, either in the beginning of a play or at the character's first entrance. Characters often talk about each other – write those descriptions down. Read your character lines out loud. Does he speak in short blunt bursts, or is he wordy? Jot down all impressions and detail from the reading – the more you put down, the more of a character profile you will have.

3) Read through the script to expose your characters wants. Other acting systems have different terminologies. Objective, super-objective, motivation are words that come to mind. Ask yourself the question "what does my character want?" There are levels of want. A want that affects his whole life, a want that affects the "play segment of his life" – that is, a want that occurs during the time span of the play, and an immediate want, say in a particular scene or moment in the play.

Here is an example: I want to be a successful provider no matter what the cost (life want), I want to feed my family today (play want) I want this piece of bread (immediate want). You may find this tedious, but it really shows in the quality of your work.

Another fictional sample of data gathering:

Author: Poor family, two brothers one sister, domineering father. Went to boarding school, became sick, left school, worked as a waiter, other menial jobs before working for a newspaper.

Character description: Tall, 45 years old, overweight, dominant personality, farmer, poor.

Other character comments: "I wish he wouldn't be so bossy!" "He really cares about us, he just doesn't know how to say it"

Wants: He wants to provide for the family no matter what the cost: when the play starts there is a drought, so he becomes a laborer. His "play" want is the same as his "life" want, but it becomes more immediate with his family's difficulty.

More notes on Character Research:
Note Taking:

Write down all that is said about your character in stage directions, dialogue, author notes. Very often these notes are written by the first stage manager of a production. Other times, certain authors are very meticulous about what they think a character appears like to others and the audience. These are not etched in stone; these can be guidelines for character portrayal.

Quick questions: Where was your character born? Where did he grow up? What kind of friends did he have? Was there an incident in your character's childhood, or later, that shaped a portion of his personality? Describe/act out that incident.

Write about your character's relationships. Are you a loner? Are you a party person? Are your relationships genuine or are they professionally motivated? What kinds of people do you like/hate? Are you domineering or more submissive?

If an animal, what would you be? Not just a "wart hog", but also an "angry, small, rough brown skinned wart hog with long tusks and a strong smelly scent"

Documentation: Write your character's back-story,

1) Real People – Number one in my book. Refer to the people watching exercise and the Persona Portfolio. Humans are the actor's library – so much good material out there to use!

2) Characters From Fiction – A character you read from a book can be a good inspiration. Allow your imagination to work with this source of inspiration, but try to keep your character real.

3) Animals – this is big with Strasberg and Adler acting techniques, and it's easy to see why. Moving like an animal gets us out of our physical comfort zone, and it makes for unique character work.

> A personal favorite – an actor working as Bagheera in Jungalbook by Edward Mast "translated" his cat licking mannerism into this meticulous sinister wiping of his stiletto. Cool.

4) Masks – almost any kind will do if it inspires you. A Fred Flintstone mask inspired a terrifying interpretation of Macbeth I once viewed. And don't have young kids around if you are wearing a clown mask.

5) Mannerisms/Body Afflictions – Twitches, lisps, slouched shoulders, a bum knee, limp.

6) Hand Properties – personal favorites are handkerchiefs, glasses, key chains, watches, bracelets, rings – all with a backstory, of course.

7) Imagination – never underestimate what your brain can come up with for inspiration.

8) Accents – work on it, though.

9) Other Interpretations – a last resort. But you can get ideas from what other people have done, just don't imitate them. It will almost always be bad work.

10) Inanimate Objects – refer to the graveyard exercise in this book to see how this could work.

11) Hats, Hair, Hair-Dos – Icing on the cake. Make this the finish to the character creation.

<u>Self-Perception Exercises</u>

When first building a character, you need to know a lot about how you present **you** as a character. In other words, what kind of a persona (the mask worn by a character) do you have as yourself? What do you look like?

First, your face. Look away from a mirror and then smile. Look back at the mirror, holding that smile. Is that what you thought your smile looked like? It took me forever to figure out that what I thought was a smile (this is all the way to college) actually looked like a smirk! Not many friends with a face like that.

Check the gamut of emotions in front of a mirror. Anger, sadness, doubt, boredom, whatever else you think you might want in your arsenal.

Phase two of this is changing what you do as a person to what your character does, and how he presents his face.

Continue on with the body. This time your hands. Practice your gestures. Again, with the emotions. Then, adapt to what you think your character would do. Use a full-length mirror for this.

Then, your stance/posture.

If you have access to a hallway, or dance room that has wall-long mirrors, check out how you walk. Learn a new walk for an exercise!

> One of the most difficult encounters I had with an actor was when I did "Phantom of the Opera." I had a lead who refused to believe he shuffled the way he did (a life of wearing flipflops.) He had to train himself to walk taller and more confident, and it took quite a while. He made it, though.

The Graveyard Exercise

Learning objective: The use of inanimate objects as character impetus.

Final product: A two-minute performance (with original script) of a persona based upon the physical characteristics of a tombstone/gravesite.

Procedure:

Observation/research: Visit a graveyard. Search for a distinctive tombstone, or a unique grave site. Write as much as you can about its appearance.

1) Is it well kept? Flowers? Clean/dirty?
2) Describe the stone itself. What materials is it made of? Marble. Coral, Slate, cement? Is it chipped, worn?
3) The name and inscription. Nationality, age of death, time period of person.

From these notes, "translate" the description into a character. You may get inspiration from the name and year born and died. There may be an impetus from the tombstone inscription. Write these new descriptions down, and use these to create and imagine a person.

Rehearsal: Use these physical descriptions to inspire the creation of a character. Practice with a voice and body appropriate to those characteristics.

Write down your monologue. Have a time, place.

On performance day, hand in your monologue, and a brief description of your tombstone and the process of creating this character.

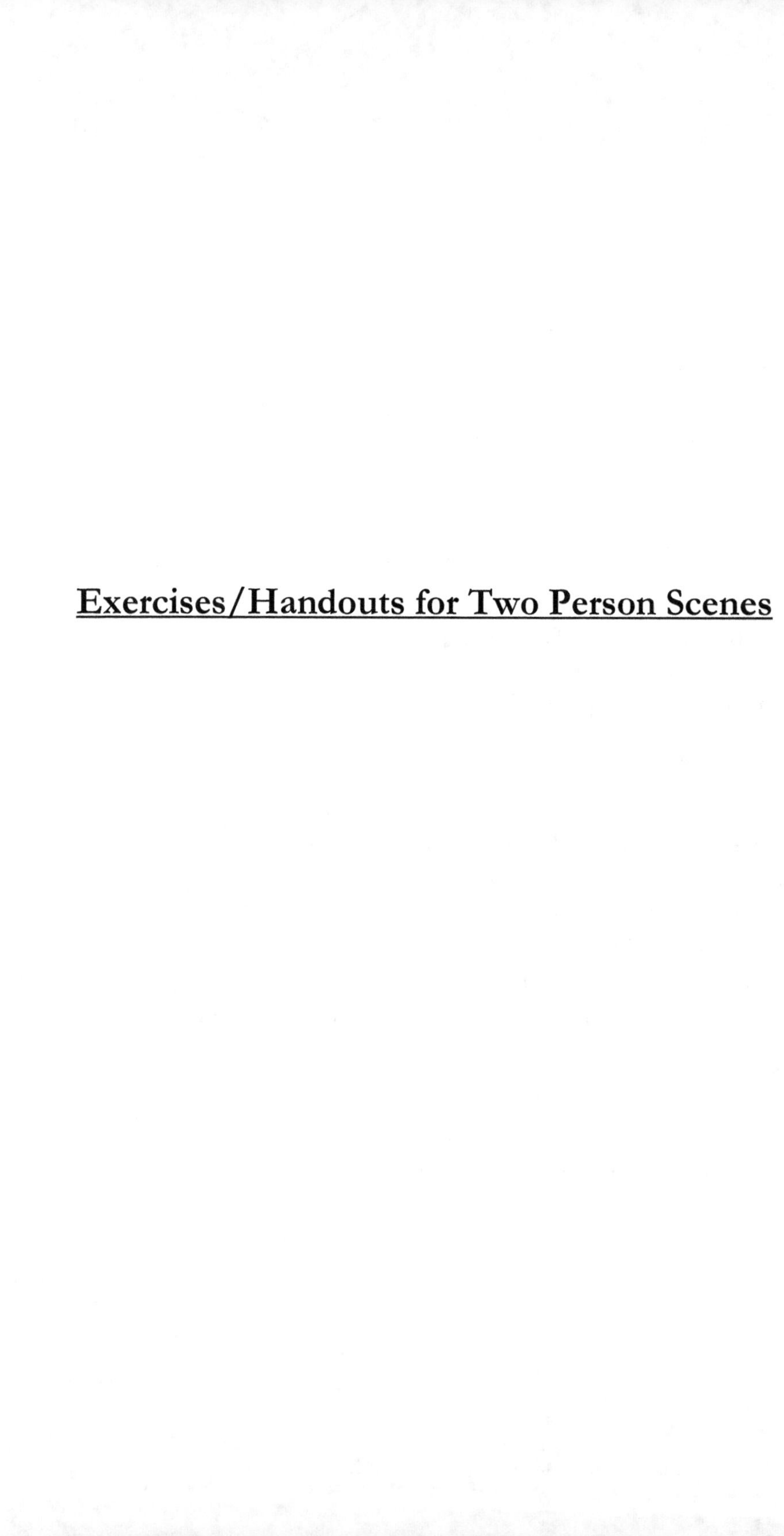

<u>Exercises/Handouts for Two Person Scenes</u>

<u>The Actor in Scene work - a check list.</u>

Script Analysis - Identifying the highs and lows of a script, discussing this with your fellow actor. Why is this scene written? What is revealed, or concealed for that matter? Who dominates the scene? Block the scene with the analysis in mind.

Working with properties – making good prop choices and giving them life and contributions (more about this in the Adler Handout.)

Costume choices – the costumes need not be accurate, but they do need to be representative of what the actual costume would do to you physically (i.e. how heavy the material is, how tight a fit it is.)

Working with fellow actors – set up your practice habits, setting up etiquette rules.

Memorizing – helping each other out!

Listening – Meisner, Meisner, Meisner (read this section!!!)

Tempo – Play with this in rehearsal. It's not about a single pace, it's how it changes. Experiment with silences.

Things to consider in scene work:
The back story
Given Circumstances
"Moments" in a scene
The Meisner, Adler, Strasberg Chekhov Methods
Proxemics

Tempo-Rhythm

A Stanislavski term. Some thoughts on its application and levels…

Tempo – the external pace   Rhythm – the internal pace

CHARACTER -- a Tempo-Rhythm determined by the type of character being portrayed. One stereotypically could say that the Tempo-Rhythm of an 80-year-old would be slower than a 15-year-old.

EMOTIONAL -- a Tempo-Rhythm about the emotional state of a character at a particular moment in time. One generally could say that the Tempo-Rhythm of an angry person would be faster than a sad one.

SCENE -- a Tempo-Rhythm determined by the interaction of characters and their responses to each other's energy and Tempo-Rhythm. An example would be a scene in which an angry person confronts a calm person: the angry person's Tempo-Rhythm would slow down, or the calm person's Tempo-Rhythm would speed up.

PLAY – a Tempo-Rhythm determined by a director's vision for a show. A generalization would be that the Tempo-Rhythm of a comedy would be faster than a tragedy.

DRAMATIC -- a Tempo-Rhythm either controlled by a director or the actors themselves. Tempo-Rhythm can create great dramatic effect – through change, moments, dialogue, silences. Although sometimes artificially created, dramatic Tempo-Rhythm is a very powerful tool for the actor.

External Tempo vs. Internal Rhythm – they need not be the same. A character could be racing internally and externally be quite calm. It is a terrific exercise to see and experiment with how this can work for the actor.

The Shadowbox Scenes:
by Michael Cristofer

Brian/Beverly
begins...
BEVERLY: Caro! Caro! You old fart!
ends...
BEVERLY: Neither did I. But it was the only way, the only way I knew.

Mark/Beverly
begins...
MARK: What am I talking about?
ends...
BEVERLY: He always cares about he wrong people.

Joe/Maggie
begins...
JOE: It would have been nice.
ends...
JOE: Don't Promise. Just come inside.

The Shadowbox Floor Plan

The Final Scene Project

You may use the floor plans/designs I have for the project, so that arranging scenes becomes easier.

Students provide the properties and costumes for their particular scene.

Rehearsals are conducted in class, and if necessary, outside of class.

I would recommend that one play be chosen. I give three options.
I would recommend August:Osage County.

August: Osage County by Tracy Letts

Act 1 Scene 2b - Jean, Johnna

Act 1 Scene 3 - Bill, Barbara

Act 2 - Barbara, Bill

Act 2 - Ivy, Violet, Mattie Fae

Act 3 Scene 1c - Barbara, Mattie Fae

Act 3 Scene 5a - Ivy, Barbara, Vi

A Streetcar Named Desire by Tennessee Williams

Scene 1 - Stella Blanche - "It's incredible how well you look Blanche."

Scene 2 - Stanley Blanche - "Hello Stanley" to "cut the rebop"

Scene 6 - Mitch Blanche - "Where's Stanley? to "I understand what that is"

Home Free by Lanford Wilson

The entire play is one male, one female. It can be divided among the class so that the play flows as one. A fun challenge.

Osage County Floor Plan

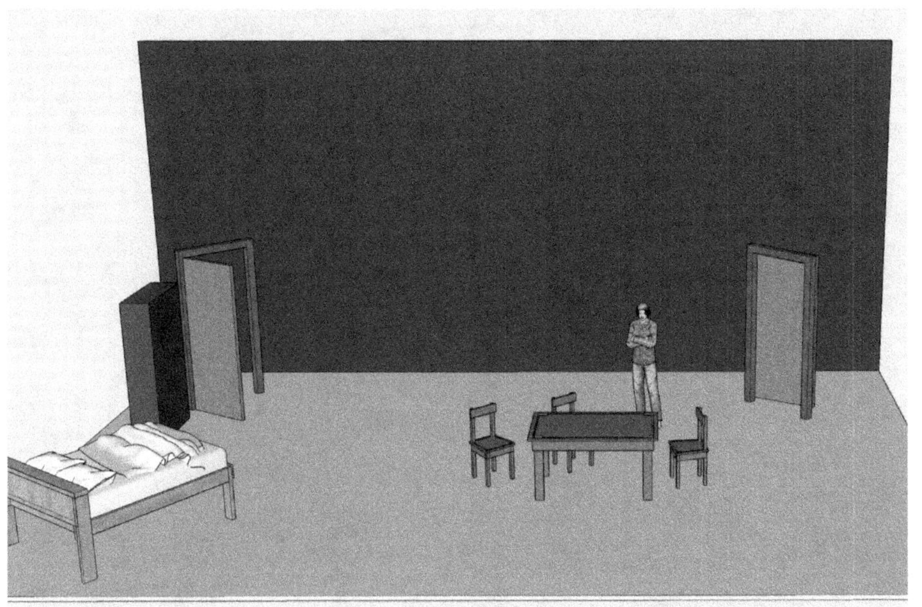

Streetcar Floor Plan

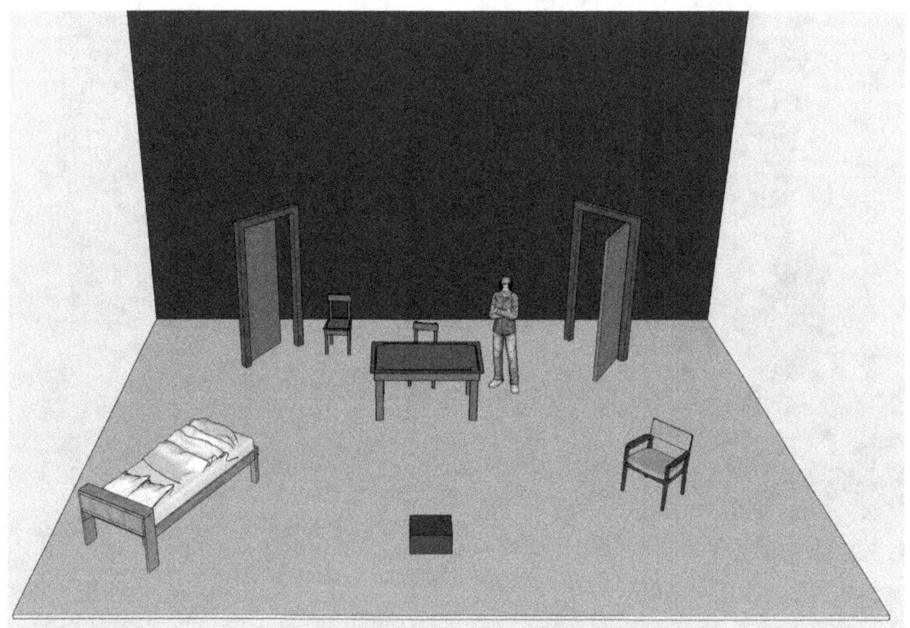

Home Free Floor Plan

Additional Classroom Teaching Material

Lee Strasberg-inspired Classroom Exercises

I use the acronym PAR for Strasberg:

"P," standing for two of his important concepts: "Private Moment," which I do not use in the classroom, and "Personal Object," which I find very useful as an acting tool.

"A," standing for "Affective Memory" (more on that below) and "Animals," which are a good source of inspiration for character development.

"R," standing for "Relaxation." Not "relaxed" in the common usage of the word. Loose, but alert. Devoid of tension would be the best definition.

Relaxation exercises:

1. Sit on a chair and release all tension. Try to find areas of the body that are still tense. Stand and do the same thing. Make this a self-awareness exercise. Tense areas of the body, release. Try to determine which areas of the body are more tense than others. Areas of special tension suggested by Strasberg: eyebrows and muscles at the temple; bridge of the nose leading to the eyes; side of the nose to the mouth and chin; behind the neck and down the back.Add more possible tension contenders: slouched shoulders; the small of the back.

2. Work with a partner to find the tense areas of your body.(In no. 1, you say "the body," here you say "your body." You need to be more consistent because it becomes distracting.) See if he sees the same tension you felt with the first exercise, or has discovered more!

1. Sight and sound. Concentrate on an object (a door, a tree, a book, a chair), then draw from memory. Put in as much detail as you can remember, down to the crack near the doorknob.

2. Taste, then more. The morning cup of coffee, orange juice, milk, the last steak eaten. Recall all the sensations, all the mental stimuli. Then, not just taste, but recall smell, sight, sound and feel. Adding the other senses adds new dimension to the experience, making it much more complete.

3. Improvisation. Next, try an improvisation based on two people reacting to the same sensations at the same time. It can be a physical activity or a sensory experience, such as seeing a ship, smelling a flower or hearing waves. They react to each other, as well as to the sensations. Keep it simple.

Sense Memory Exercises:

These exercises are simple, but very beneficial to the actor. You instantly can spot the actor faking the sip of cup of coffee or the swig of liquor.

1. Having a breakfast drink, whatever it may be.
2. Looking in the mirror, what I call "the morning ritual."
3. Getting dressed and undressed (careful here!), all done in pantomime.
4. Recalling three pieces of material – silk, cotton, wool, whatever.
5. Feeling the sunshine on your face. Love this one!
6. Feeling a sharp pain. Be specific with this one: headache, toothache, stepping on a sharp object. What happens to the whole body, not just the part that is being hurt?
7. Experiencing a sharp taste and sharp smell. Another winner. I love to watch actors simulate that bite into a lime or react to smelling gasoline.

8. Recalling a memorable place and using as many senses to explain why it was so memorable.

9. Simulating situations that affect the whole body – a bath, a shower or a sauna; a windy day; a rainstorm; a cold winter day with not enough clothing or a very hot summer day.

The Personal Object – a very successful exercise in my classes to stimulate emotion. This is essentially an "Affective Memory" exercise using a physical object to inspire a memory.

Students are asked to bring to class an object with which they have a strong emotional attachment. Classroom chairs are set up in a circle, and students relate why the objects are so special to them. Many events tied to the objects are especially sad, but they don't need to be.

The end result of this exercise is two-fold: First, the vulnerability aspect. Actors talking about a personal event are vulnerable, revealing something only they know about, and asking the audience to understand, listen to and, possibly, empathize with. It's a big step for a performer to do this. Second, it's a great acting tool. Having the object with them during a scene can get an actor to laugh or cry!

What is a **"Private Moment?"** This concept takes the personal object idea even further. The actor "does" -- not "performs" -- a very personal and private moment in class. It can make many class members uncomfortable, especially those watching. Inevitably, a participant will giggle due to being uncomfortable, and that would be very difficult for the performer to take.

Affective Memory – in this exercise, the actor recreates the stimuli present during an emotional event in his own life. He tries to re-experience the specific stimuli, instead of simply recalling the event or remembering the emotion. He seeks to recapture the specific sights, smells, sounds and tactile sensations that provoked the emotions.

The actor just beginning to do "Affective Memory" exercises should choose an unusual event in his past, albeit not too dramatic an event. Although traumatic events are not specifically asked for, the incidents chosen often are. The experience need not be traumatic to be useful. The final outcome of the affective memory may turn out to have little obvious relation to the original occurrence; the result may be far different than what was expected. The actor may laugh when he originally cried or vice versa. However, if the response is a useful one, it becomes an important affective memory to store in the actor's repertoire.

Here are exercises to go about it gently, lastly incorporating "Affective Memory" into a scene:
1. Learning to relax. Relaxation is important. Beginners sometimes take an hour to relax; experienced actors, 20-30 minutes. The actor concentrates on experiencing his five senses in a particular situation.
2. Working with a personal object, taking exercise one to a higher level, and using affective memory at the same time. A high level of concentration is emphasized.
Now we try and include the scene:
3. After creating the emotion, the actor speaks out the scene using his own words. A physical task may be incorporated into the scene.
4. Using lines of dialogue from a scene.
5. Practicing affective memory work, unsupervised, without a teacher or partner. In the process, the actor builds a library of affective memory tools.

Notes on Michael Chekhov

The Chekhov acronym is VIA, for Veil, Imagination and Atmosphere:

Veil – the mask or persona worn by an actor. This can be as simple as a change in the actor's vocal range, a lisp, a limp or a complete makeover, with costume, properties and make-up involved.

Imagination – instead of experience. Chekhov was big on the idea that if an actor did not have a memory to evoke emotions (Stanislavski's emotion recall), he could use imagination to evoke the emotion.

Atmosphere – defined as "the source of moods and waves of feeling that emanate from one's surroundings." But it's more than that.

I like to think of "Atmosphere" as Stanislavski's circumstances, plus sense memory, rolled into one. Smell and taste transport me. I can smell a cup of coffee and get transported to another time and place. One of my favorite film moments is from the Disney animation, Ratatouille, where the Peter O'Toole critic tastes the Ratatouille, zooming him back in time to his happy and more innocent youth.

There are different levels of atmosphere:
"Holy" atmosphere – brought about by place and the aura of a place. Some clear examples, each with its own special aura, are churches, cemeteries, hospitals, carnivals and boardrooms.

"Emotional" atmosphere – such as love, anger, sadness. These often are created by specific events: a wedding (love), a funeral (sadness).

"Persona" atmosphere – an aura from a particular character in a play, or even the aura of a famous person, changes the atmosphere in a situation.

Case in point: my Theatre Performance class was discussing a scene just rehearsed from "Twelfth Night," when who should be at the rear classroom door but a star from the TV series, "Lost," which was being filmed in Hawaii. He was intrigued by the discussion, walked into the room upon invitation and gave a short talk about his work with "Shakespeare in the Park" while a master's student at NYU. Talk about atmosphere! The class was in awe a good 30 minutes after he left.

Atmosphere Exercises

Group exercises: Improvisation
Have groups of four or five improvise a scene at these various locations:

1. At a fair or carnival, looking for friends who are late. Focus primarily on the sights, sounds and smells of the location.
2. At a hospital, where a close friend is in ICU. Guide students by helping them "see" where they are and smell that hospital smell.
3. Late night on a dare at a cemetery. What is heard, seen, imagined, smelled. One person gets separated from the group.
4. A tour of a famous cathedral. Someone chooses this moment to express his love for another member of the group.

Through the door:

Have a door set up at center stage, or just have an imaginary door.

The performer is to go from one familiar atmosphere to another. For example: in a bedroom, alone, talking to a friend on the phone, then joining family at dinner. Or, outside talking with friends, then going to final exam in a classroom.

With a pair of performers: a bar waitresses in the kitchen, complaining about customers, then serving drinks to those very customers; or a boy and girl on a date, outside a restaurant, then entering to discover it's a biker bar.

Have participants create their own scenes with "atmospheres."

<u>**Some wisdom from Stella Adler**</u> (quotes are hers. Most of the exercises here are variations on her exercises found in her book "The Technique of Acting")

The Adler acronym is CIA.
Circumstances – which is essentially Stanislavski's given circumstances – the who, what, why, where and when of a scene. Stella is big on where, and that should always be the first to work on.
Imagination – some Stanislavski and some Chekhov influence. She takes it up another notch though, so check out the imagination exercises below.
Action – Activity – simple and brilliant. The actor needs to identify the action of a scene, and the activities used for that action create justified action. Examples below. It can get a little tricky with semantics on this one, so try and keep your understanding of this concept simple. A can also mean animals, as they are used as an exercise for flexibility (and imagination, too!).

"Acting is stubborn work, necessitating constant attention and a rigorous schedule. It is not for geniuses. It is for people who work step by step."

"There is a difference between the truth of life and the truth of the theatre. And you must learn not to mix them up. You are going to learn to express yourself in size."

Actors need to set up their own goals at the start of a learning session, or a semester. Be honest as you list assets and faults. Confer with a fellow learner that you know well, who can be honest with you. Set up strategies and schedules to fix the problems. List possible people who can help!

<u>**Exercises to start you off:**</u>

Exercise: understanding the **energy** of the voice
Read aloud an editorial, or a sports column, a blog every day. Read or speak ten, fifteen, twenty, fifty and a hundred feet from someone to hear your true range. Read as if the audience were across the table, across the room, across the street.

The exercise above may appear easier than it is. It is important that the quality of the sound in reading remains the same regardless of the distance.

Exercise: **Tension**
Locate areas of tension of the body. Relax the whole body except one hand. Put all the tension into that one hand. Sit, stand, and walk around in that state.

Adler is big into what you can do physically to help create character and this is an example of one. A character could be created from a person who has a stiff knee. That one physical trait can create an interesting character, or at least be a good start!

Exercise: **Physical Controls**

For the body:
Make a stiff knee, and control it by letting nothing else stiffen. Walk around. Walk up steps. Dress with it. Dance with it. Do the same with a sore back, or a broken ankle. Keep the second and third finger straight as if in a splint. Give yourself a job to do - clean the kitchen. Put on an apron.

For the Voice: Practice a lisp: use some of the tongue twisters located in the voice appendix.

Exercise: **Muscular Memory Of A Prop**
Exercise: clean dirty eyeglasses. Glasses bent, straighten. Glasses broken, fix.

Exercise: a jar's lid is too tight. Remember the muscular energy needed to open it. Repeat.

Exercise: needle and thread. At first, use real props. Then use your imagination to create scenarios using an imaginary prop. The needle gets snagged in thick cloth. The needle breaks. The hole in the needle is way too small for your thread, but you stubbornly persist.

Exercise: **Animal Movement**

Exercise: Perform an animal you like. Observe. Try and imitate the movement as best you can. Exercise your animal 15 minutes a day. Focus first on movement, then sound. Then, put the animals in a place - monkey in a zoo, bear in a cage, cat in a living room.

Exercises in imagination:

Exercise: Clothes in your closet. Describe, in detail, from memory. Try to do that with another imaginary wardrobe closet. Be as detailed as your real closet. This is difficult, and needs practice.

Exercise: The view out the window. Teacher describes a view out a second story window. After the description, the student draws the view. Have students compare their work.

Exercise: walking along a country road, look at the sky, blue. White clouds are drifting by and birds are flying in formation. A long fence, along a meadow. A cow. Green grass. A small creek. A bridge. Make it yours, personal.

Exercise: walking down a lane. A long branch of a tree has been cut off. Go up a small road. The grass is quite high. Wooden bridge. A pond. Small fish in the pond. Further down the road is a yard with a clothesline tied between two trees. Cloths hanging. Pajamas, socks, sneakers, tablecloth, overalls. Ask yourself - how tall was the grass? How was the bridge made, what did it look like? Describe the sneakers, the tablecloth, the overalls.

Quick Concentration:

Exercise: Concentrate on seeing rapidly. Go to a bookstore or a supermarket, and see as much as you can in 10 seconds. Write down all you saw. Observe what your acting partner is wearing and see as much as you can in five seconds. Look away, and write what you have seen. Go to a bus stop. A shopping center.

"The actor sees and acts in imaginative circumstances. This is not hard if you accept that everything you imagine is truthful. The actor's job is to defictionalize the fiction. If you need a lemon tree but have never seen one, you will imagine some kind of lemon tree. You will accept it as if you have seen it. You have imagined it; therefore it exists. Anything that goes through the imagination has a right to live and has its own truth."

Exercises in Circumstance:

"Where am I?" is the first question you must ask yourself when you go on the stage. Relaxation comes from your recognition of the truthfulness of the circumstances. Onstage, you are never actually in lifelike circumstances, but you must accept them as such.

Words do not make the play. If you first go into the words, you will not be a modern actor – just a bad one.

If you really act, the joy is in the doing of it. Any actor who is on the stage and knows what it is like to experience the circumstances would not trade that experience for any other.

Living in circumstances

Exercise: action is to dress. Dress in a dressing room in a theatre. Dress in your bedroom. Dress in a locker room of a gym.

Exercise: in the circumstances of a restaurant, the action is to order dinner. Go to the bar and get a drink. Get to your table and order dinner. Go to the checkroom and get your coat.

Build the larger circumstance

Where does the action take place? When? What time of day, season. Build a place for yourself. Begin to live in the place as the character. What city/town? Country?

Action is something you do. To cook.
Action has an end. I'm cooking an omelet.
Action is done in circumstances. I'm cooking at my mother's house.

Action is justified. I'm cooking to feed my family.
In an action, you must know what you are doing, where you are doing it, when you are doing it, why you are doing it.

Activity is the detail of the action.

exercise: action: cooking that omelet

         activities: crack six eggs, beat them, add a bit of cream cheese . Slice mushrooms, onions. Simmer the onions and mushrooms in butter. Set aside. Grease a non-stick pan. Cook the eggs at medium heat, and add the mushrooms and onions in the center when it starts to harden. Fold over the two sides. Flip over the omelet to finish. (Hey, this omelet should be pretty good!)

More Action Activity Exercises:

Actions are listed below. Add activities to the action.

listening to music   loading a rifle
baking a cake   sewing a button
making a bed   putting on a dress
changing a tire   ironing

An action is sometimes not completed. Action can be changed by the circumstances in the scene, or by another characters action.

A personal favorite of this very concept: Scene two from "A Streetcar named Desire." Blanche walks out of a hot shower, in a see-through slip, with every intention of getting dressed to go out to dinner with her sister that night. Stanley, on the other hand, is waiting for her in the room to ask her about what she has done to lose Stella's (and now his) inheritance. Blanche stops at the bathroom door, and in that one instant, sees the handsome, rough man her sister has married, and decides to seduce him.

Other examples of action not being completed, or being interrupted:
Action: taking a bath. No hot water. You dress instead.
Action: going to the theatre. Doorbell rings. You welcome your guest. Go to the theatre.
Action: studying anatomy. Telephone rings. Close the window. Turn off the radio. Adjust the clock. Get a cup of coffee. Go back to studying anatomy.
Action: make coffee. Mailman rings the bell. Telephone rings. Dog wants to go out. Make coffee.

The concept of "as if" – I like this one.
As a performer you are often asked to express emotion, pain, shock, dying, or other experiences you may have no knowledge of. These are actions for which you will need a task.
An example:
Pain – a headache. There are many types of headaches. Here are four

possible ways of expressing this pain physically: Imagine "as if" someone was pushing in your eyeball. "As if" you were making a hole in your eyes. As if you were sticking a needle in your eye. As if you were pouring strong alcohol in your eyes to clean them.

Muscular Challenges

Choose a simple everyday activity, such as making a bed. The Muscular challenge adds or "colors" the activity.

Challenges:	sore ribs/difficulty breathing	sprained ankle
	headache(define)	sore lower back
	toothache	chest pains
	sore knees	sore neck
	sore feet	pain in the side
	sore shoulder	sore butt
	painful joints	dry cough

Try to find a muscular challenge that will aid your monologue.

"The foundation of acting is the reality of doing."
"Acting is living under imaginary circumstances"
"The truth of ourselves is the root of our acting."

The acronym for Meisner is PRIM. The definitions and exercises you read here are inspired by the classes being taught at the Meisner school, with a personal take on most all of them.

P - for Preparation - the device that permits you to start your scene or play in a condition of emotional aliveness. Preparation only happens for the first moment of the scene, and then you never know what's going to happen. Use your imagination or recall to give yourself an impulse that moves you, and you alone. Preparation is a warming up process. Warning: do not indicate the emotion, just use it to stimulate you.

R - for Repetition – this process is tedious, and difficult for young performers to understand. "Why are we just repeating what they are saying – what is the point?" Persist. The actors finally get it, and when they do, they are astonished at how simple yet important this exercise is. More later.

I - for Independent Activity (IA), and Impulse. There is often confusion with Meisner's IA and Adler's Action – activity and rightly so. I like to differentiate the two by the conditions involved in Meisner's IA. More later.

M – for memorizing in monotone. Actors are given a script and are to memorize it and repeat it over with no feeling. Keep it neutral - open to any influence. The word "monotone" often means "robotic" to the actors, and that's a no-no. Another problem arises in that monotone often makes them speed up the lines – again, don't do it. I believe in this concept. Many actors memorize in their particular speech patterns, and don't deviate from that memorized pattern. It doesn't work when the line they are reacting to suggests saying their line differently.

Those little words in parenthesis underneath the character's name in the script like 'softly, angrily, entreatingly' should be erased immediately because they are premeditated and are not intuitive.

Starting out exercises: Listening

Exercise one – listen in the classroom. Listen for particular things - cars, birds, and people's voices. How many did you hear? Discuss in class.

Exercise two – the listening game. A bit of preparation beforehand: cut (out of card stock) five shapes with five different colors – a green triangle, a blue rectangle, a yellow square, a white circle, and a red octagon. Every participant has a set of these shapes. They sit in groups (three or four) on the floor with their backs to each other. A player arranges the shapes in front of him. He then describes the pattern he has created. "The red octagon is beside the green triangle, and the blue rectangle is placed on top of both of them (and so on)" Other group participants may not ask questions – they are just to listen and recreate the pattern. It's over when he's done describing the pattern. They look to see if they copied the player's pattern. It's a simple game that really is a metaphor for a play if you think about it – actors say their lines, and the audience can't ask questions, there is no rewind, no instant replay. Communication is key! The game continues with all in the group leading at some point.

Repetition exercises: Two players (A, B) stand about 4 feet away from each other, hands on sides, relaxed.
A looks at B and states a fact about B. No negatives, no snide comments. B repeats what A says EXACTLY.

A: "You have black hair" B: "You have black hair"

The two of them repeat this over and over again.

A: "You have black hair" B: "You have black hair" A: "You have black hair" B: "You have black hair"

If they are good, nothing ever changes, and this is the goal in the beginning: learning how to hear your acting partner's tone -EXACTLY. Down to the pauses, the breath, the tone, the tempo, the pitch. Let the class judge if it's exact, not just you the teacher. Reverse the order, with B commenting on A.

B: "Your hair is curly" A: "Your hair is curly" and so on.

2) Repetition with personalization, or acknowledgement. This is pretty much the same as the first exercise, but now the second player acknowledges the comment:

A: "You have black hair" B: "I have black hair" A: "You have black hair" B: "I have black hair"
A: "You have black hair" B: "I have black hair" A: "You have black hair" B: "I have black hair"

Again, reverse the order. B comments, A acknowledges the comment.

3) Repetition, acknowledgement, and impulse comment, and acknowledgment. Here is where it gets a little tricky. You've learned phase one and two, now phase three calls upon another of Meisner's concepts – impulse. You continue with the repetition until an impulse bubbles up in you to make a comment about the other person.

A: "You have black hair" B: "I have black hair" A: "You have black hair" B: "I have black hair"
A: "You have black hair" B: "I have black hair" A: "You have black hair" B: "Your hair is curly"
A: "My hair is curly" B: "Your hair is curly" A: "My hair is curly" B: "Your hair is curly"
A: "My hair is curly" B: "Your hair is curly" A: "My hair is curly" B: "Your hair is curly"

Have the whole class do these exercises.

Instinct - spontaneous, impulsive reaction to the moment.

Player goes offstage. Player thinks of a given circumstance that he is coming from – say, there was a fire down the block. He recalls the event and how it affects him emotionally, walks to the door and knocks.

Practice with these other scenarios, then make up some of your own. Coming home from a tragedy at a hospital. A new year's party, and he kissed the girl of his dreams. Just flunked a final exam. Just read a letter from his parents – they are getting a divorce.
Again, have all in the class practice this exercise.

The Independent Activity, and this is a biggie.

First, conditions of the Independent Activity. I use the acronym BIDE. The activity must be Believable in the play's circumstances, Immediate (or urgent, got to do this NOW), it must be Difficult to do and it must be Evident (tangible to the teacher and audience, for that matter)

Here's an example of an IA with problems: A student will come in with "I am solving Pi in my head." It may be believable in the play's circumstances, it's difficult, and you'd have to put in conditions as to why it's urgent, but the big problem is that we have no idea if he really is solving Pi in his head. If he wrote his solving it, it could change things, because we can see the math and the process happening on a piece of paper.

Here's a sample IA –
An accountant is solving the tally for the day's sales in a department store. He has five minutes till the auditor arrives. He will lose his job if the numbers don't add up. He becomes aware as he's solving the math that someone is cheating the store, and he has to find out who in that short time.

In the class, have actors come in with possible IAs as homework. The discussion should first be if the work they submit is a legitimate IA. When working on scenes, have actors create IAs for their scene. Some will be harder than others.

And now we combine the three concepts together.

Two players. A is offstage, behind the door. He's busy doing his **preparation** (remember what that was?) B is onstage at a desk working on his **Independent Activity**. Call "curtain" to get B going on his IA (let's use my accountant one from above) Now call "go!" to A, who walks to the door and knocks. A enters, walks to the desk. B comments on the quality of the knock on the door (but cannot stop the work of his IA!!!), and A acknowledges it. Let's say A came from the fire.
B: "That was an urgent knock" A: "That was an urgent knock" B: "That was an urgent knock" A: "That was an urgent knock" B: "That was an urgent knock" A: "That was an urgent knock"

A comments on the quality with which B is working on his IA when the impulse moves him. Let's say a minute later A bubbles up with something and B acknowledges it.

A: "You're writing fast" B: "I'm writing fast"
A: "You're writing fast" B: "I'm writing fast"
A: "You're writing fast" B: "I'm writing fast"
A: "You're writing fast" B: "I'm writing fast"

Master the exercise above, using different IAs and of course, different preparations, and have all class members try being A or B.

Whew! You're done! But wait… It gets more complicated.

Finally, we put all of this together with the scene you are working on.

A is the character Joe from The Shadowbox. B is Maggie. Joe has come from offstage, where he's been gazing at the sunset, bringing this sense of peace with him (preparation). Maggie is frantic looking through her picture book – she remembers tucking in a hundred-dollar bill on a page that she saved for Steve, their son – where is it? She wants to give it to him, but the stupid pages keep getting stuck, the book is old and frazzled. Joe knocks at the gate.
Maggie: "That was a quiet knock" Joe: "That was a quiet knock"
Maggie: "That was a quiet knock" Joe: "That was a quiet knock"
Maggie: "That was a quiet knock" Joe: "That was a quiet knock"
Maggie: "That was a quiet knock"
Joe: "You're ripping the pages" Maggie: "I'm ripping the pages"
Joe: "You're ripping the pages" Maggie: "I'm ripping the pages"
Joe: "You're ripping the pages" Maggie: "I'm ripping the pages"
and finally, the scene starts with
Joe: "It would have been nice"
Maggie: "What?"

The scene goes on, with Maggie still at her IA. She can stop when she wants, but the work has been done.

And what work is that, you may ask? One of the most phenomenal things that happen in the Meisner technique is that an actor stops "acting" and just Does. The actor playing Maggie is so preoccupied with the IA at hand that she responds impulsively to what Joe gives her. She's busy, and she is doing something real.

<u>This is important: The actor needs to pick up the impulse of the line delivered to you, rather than the cue. The actor does wait for the cue, but the impulse, the emotion, comes whenever it's felt. Learn the lines, but trust and respond to the impulses.</u>

A nice Meisner metaphor - the text is like a canoe and the river, which it floats on, is the emotion and subtext.

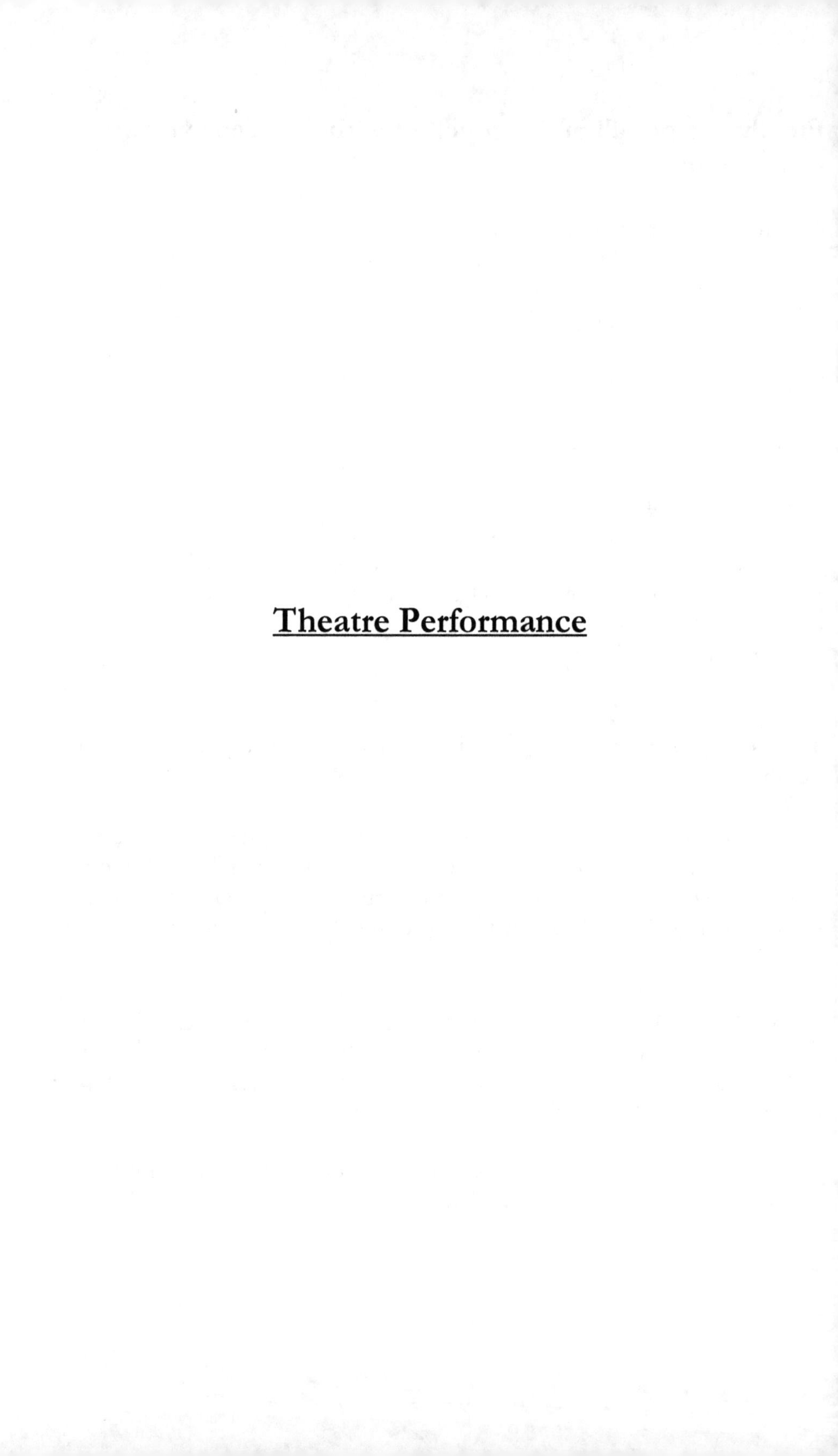

Theatre Performance

Here are some of your assumptions as teacher for this class:
1) The students are responsible for the production aspects of this show. They not only act, but they are given additional responsibilities in production, which can include, but is not limited to: 1) Publicity 2) Program 3) Props 4) Set painting and construction 5) Lighting 6) Sound 7) Costumes..
They are not responsible for casting, directing nor design (some students have designed however!) – that is your job.

2) This class is not necessarily offered every semester, as it is based on enrollment. There was a year that the course was offered only one semester, and it was a small show. And yet another semester, there were two Theatre Performance classes, and we offered three full one acts in successive weeks!

3) It is important for you to have knowledge of the demographics of the class as soon as you can. Say you find out that there are 6 women and 3 men in your class: you then have to research 6 women; 3 men plays for class review.

4) Theatre Performance is a democracy. You as a teacher provide your pre-approved scripts for the class to read, and then the fun begins. The plays are presented by class members as to why they should or shouldn't be produced. Then, plays are exchanged, and the debate continues. There have been semesters where plays were chosen after two class meetings, others took about nine class meetings.

5) The play is chosen by class vote. Auditions are done by read-throughs of the script. After this, each class member writes down what role they would like to work on. I email my cast list to the class, so that the actors can be emotional at home.

6) The Production begins, in all aspects. Production jobs are assigned, acting is rehearsed in class, and set building is after class and weekends.

7) The performance day approaches. About a month before opening, I generally hold additional rehearsals after school hours and weekends if necessary. When tech week comes along, about one to two weeks before opening night, longer technical rehearsals happen.

8) The show happens. The show closes. The class strikes the set, does a post-production review, submits their final evaluation paper, and the semester is over.

Hand out the portfolio requirements, or make sure each student has an electronic copy. Supply your email address.

Discuss the work ethic handout .
Discuss student expectations of the class.
Discuss a little bit about the history of the productions that have been done, and some of the challenges.

Review stage blocking annotation, and expectations during blocking work.

Review stage movement, on the stage, one by one. You'd be surprised the knowledge that has slipped through the cracks.

By the end of class, hand out the scripts. One script per class member. I try not to have duplicates.

> Here's a touchy subject: I have, over the years, been very protective of my personal life. Lately, however, I have found the best way to communicate with my students is texting. I give my personal phone number to them. This has saved so much time! Especially with rehearsals. So far, they have been very responsible about this. No prank calls, etc. – cross my fingers…

The second class meeting, have a blackboard in front of the class with the script titles and these categories:

Plot – Easy, difficult to follow? Interesting? Why?
Characters – are these good characters to portray? Is responsibility evenly distributed?
Theme – Do you believe what the play says, is about?
Practical Considerations – Can this work in the space we have? Do we have the time to build it?
The Audience – Does this play work for our High School and Adult audiences? Too mature? To simple?
Finally, could/should we do this play?

Have each student rank (scale of one to ten, ten being high) the categories above, and write on the board as they make their presentation. It usually is pretty subjective, so keep the questions from other class members as objective as possible. This continues until a play has been decided.

Before I even list what I expect of you, here are some assumptions:
BE ON TIME AND READY TO START. NO GUM ONSTAGE. WEAR
SHOES PLEASE. ALWAYS HAVE YOUR SCRIPTS (PAPER, PLEASE!) AND
PENCILS WITH ERASERS. NO TALKING BACKSTAGE – RESPECT THE
WORK ONSTAGE.

1) The show is cast, the blocking starts. As soon as a scene is blocked, I expect you
to have the scene memorized. This will be graded. Doing memory work gradually
(as opposed to cramming near the end) is key to our success this semester.

2) The actor is responsible for his/her own props. It means you are in charge of
getting either the actual prop you will use or its size and weight equivalent. Use this
as early as possible in the rehearsal process. The prop should become a tool for
you, not an encumbrance. **Miming props is a no-no, it develops awful stage
habits.**

3) The actor develops his/her own warm-up routine. I am a firm believer in this.
While group warm-ups are good for ensemble, they can often overextend the actor's
voice if s/he is not careful. Warm-ups should start with flexibility and concentration
exercises, and gradually build up in intensity, approximating the kind of energy you
will need for your performance. Do not learn a warm-up routine opening night.
Develop a unique warm up routine for every show that you do!

4) The actor arrives early in the theatre, checks exits and entrances in the
performance space, walks through the show mentally and physically before the
performance happens. You will find stuck doors, nails on the floor, missing props,
chewing gum on your seat, all kinds of things like that. Find that all out before you
start the show and mess up your lines because things aren't where they are supposed
to be. If they aren't, it's **your** fault and nobody else's.

5) On performance evenings, develop a way to stay focused on the play and each
other as characters. Do not get too distracted by your nervousness (which shows in
so many ways!) Find a way to relax your nerves, run through the play in your mind. I
personally find it helpful to have your script in the dressing room with me. It's a
comfort – like a good luck charm.

A Streetcar Named Desire by Tennessee Williams. Powerful, and a challenge for high school students. The actors will never look the age they are portraying, but it is always about the challenge and them trying. A very satisfying experience for a director.

Arsenic And Old Lace by Joseph Kesselring. You will have so much fun with this one. Hilarious characters. This play is timeless. The opening is a bit long and wordy, but can be fixed with the character Teddy going crazy on the set.

August: Osage County by Tracy Letts. I know, the language is really strong, and it is three hours, but the play is visceral. If you have the actor talent, do it. Taking risks is what we do, after all.

Blithe Spirit by Noel Coward. The set for this is a little tricky, especially for the final scene. But Madame Arcati is a tour de force role, and young women love to play the bickering wives for some reason. So much fun to direct, though there is much precision needed in the blocking.

The Crucible by Arthur Miller. Powerful story and powerful characters. Keep the costumes and set simple and focus on the acting.

The Foreigner by Larry Shue. Five males, two females. Absolutely the funniest play ever. Brilliantly written. Great characters. Best for smaller theatres.

The Glass Menagerie by Tennessee Williams. Two males, two females who are strong actors needed. Lyrical, powerful and quite sad. Amanda Wingfield is a tough role to play for a high school student, and Tom isn't far behind.

The Hot l Baltimore by Lanford Wilson. The play starts slow, but it picks up about five minutes in and never lets go. A wonderful ensemble piece about a hotel about to be torn down, with great earthy characters who live in it – three prostitutes, ol' deaf Mr. Morse, wise old Millie, and riff-raff customers for the night. The hotel staff is great! The dialogue is brilliant.

The Importance Of Being Earnest by Oscar Wilde. Great for a smaller venue. Witty, charming, and the female characters are so much fun and smart! The male parts are not too shabby either – you'll need a charmer to play Algernon!!

<u>The Laramie Project</u> by Moises Kauffman and the Tectonic Project. This is difficult, yet powerful, based on the true story of the killing of Matthew Shepherd in Laramie, Wyoming. The cast was originally eight (four males, four females) and they played an average of six roles each. Do the math; the possibilities of a small-to-very-large cast is how many parts an actor gets.

<u>Laundry And Bourbon</u> by James McClure. A 45-minute one act that is normally preceded by **Lone Star** which is a bit racy for high school, but Laundry isn't. Beautiful three-woman show, set on a porch on a hot Texas afternoon. Love this one. Great for intimate theatre.

<u>The Shadowbox</u> by Michael Cristofer. Four males, four females. Three families in a hospice, and their beautiful, tragic stories. The characters are fabulous. A mature play, with some suggestive language.

<u>Stand And Deliver</u> by Robert Bella. This is a very good ensemble show, especially for high school actors – it is about them after all. Based on the true story of Jaime Escalante coming to East Los Angeles in the early 1980s to teach math to inner city Chicano kids. The play is better than the movie because it focuses on the kids 'lives rather than Escalante's. The monologues in the play are quite powerful.

<u>Steel Magnolias</u> by Robert Harling. Six females. Wonderful characters. Single set, a beauty salon. Southern accents would be nice. Best in a small performance space.

<u>You Can't Take It With You</u> by Moss Hart and George Kauffman. A charming classic that has wonderful characters, lines and a huge message. Single set, props galore, accents, explosives, printing presses, and so on – simply a riot!

Chekhov One Acts – suggested pieces are: **<u>The Marriage Proposal, The Festivities</u>**, and most of all, **<u>The Bear</u>**. Please use the Paul Schmidt translation, as the dialogue is so good. This makes a delightful evening of theatre.

And of course, any Shakespeare you have the time to do, because you need the time to do it well.

Suggested Children's Theatre Plays (With Notes)

The Arkansaw Bear by Aurand Harris. A moving play about death told in an optimistic way. Young Ellie's grandfather is dying and she can't cope. She escapes to her "fantasy" tree, and meets an imaginary character, the Arkansaw Bear, who has troubles facing his own death. Casting of the young girl is an important consideration. Cast of six, and genders are interchangeable. **Dramatic Publishing Company.**

How To Eat Like A Child by Delia Ephron, John Foster, Judith Kahan. MUSICAL. A cast of 15, with only two or three being necessarily male or female. A series of vignettes, ranging from "How to torture your sister" to "How to ask for a dog." Minimal sets and properties, but good singing, acting and <u>enthusiasm</u> a must. **Samuel French.**

Jungalbook by Edward Mast. A cast of 8-12 people, with doubling. The "jungal" is the modern urban jungle, and the characters are humans with animal-like characteristics. There are very good set, costume and lighting possibilities with this show. An excellent retelling of the Kipling classic. **Dramatic Publishing Company.**

Liza And The Riddling Cave by John Urquhart. Cast of five males, five females, with extras if needed. An enchanting story of a young girl who can't talk, but she does have a lot to say, and she's smart – especially with riddles. There are set challenges, and the lighting should be special to convey the mysterious "ice mountain." **Dramatic Publishing Company.**

Mother Hicks by Susan Zeder. Cast of four men and four women who create 10 characters. A very good dramatic acting show for an older children audience. Different locations around Ware, Illinois in the 1930s. **Dramatic Publishing Company.**

Wiley And The Hairy Man by Susan Zeder. A cast of eight-nine, with two males needed. The technical aspects of this show can be very challenging, especially if the director wants to establish the Louisiana swamp. The Hairy Man, Mammy and Wiley are wonderful parts. The Swamp Chorus is essential in creating the eerie swamp feeling. **Dramatic Publishing Company.**

Suggested Musicals to Perform

The Fantasticks by Tom Jones, Harvey Schmidt. The best small cast show. Fathers can become mothers, if you transpose. The Gallo, Matt and Luisa parts must be excellent singers/actors. Great for small theatre spaces. Single set, the simpler the better.

Godspell by John Michael Tebelak, Stephen Schwartz.
Your best bet if you enjoy directing using improvisation techniques, and have the actors who enjoy this theatre type. Great songs, and opportunities for great dancing if you have the people for it. Very adaptable in terms of cast size.

Into the Woods by James Lapine and Stephen Sondheim.
The music is tough, but hey, it's Sondheim. And he's just the greatest composer/lyricist there is. Great roles and opportunities for singer/actors. Dancing is minimal, and could be simple. The songs are just fabulous.

Man of La Mancha by Dale Wasserman.
Wonderful character parts, and great songs and a great message. Excellent single set design possibilities. The stage combat is tricky. Cervantes needs to be played by a very dynamic actor.

Oliver! by Lionel Bart. Somehow this show is very popular and on people's "favorite musical" list. The book is bad, but the music is endearing, and the lead roles are very dynamic. Use a unit set.

Pippin by Roger Hirson, Stephen Schwartz.
An underrated show, and a great learning experience for actor/singers. There is more to the script than the surface, and the study of the Fosse production would benefit your show concept greatly. The choreography is tough, and it would be great if you have a Fosse trained choreographer. Expandable cast.

All the plays chosen work well for a smaller theatre.

Some suggestions for a class format:

1 ½ hour class time.

15 minutes warmup, 15 minutes review/set up
45-minute rehearsal, 15-minute review/discuss/take down

Some classroom "musts"

a lockable properties cabinet.
a portable sound machine (for warmups, music in the show, etc.)

Suggested properties to have permanently:

Place setting for six (knives, spoons, forks, plates, glasses)
          (unbreakable if possible)
Books, magazines, newspapers, writing implements
Chairs, benches, a bed, bookcase, table, desk, a movable stand up door
Stools, couch (if possible) Side tables

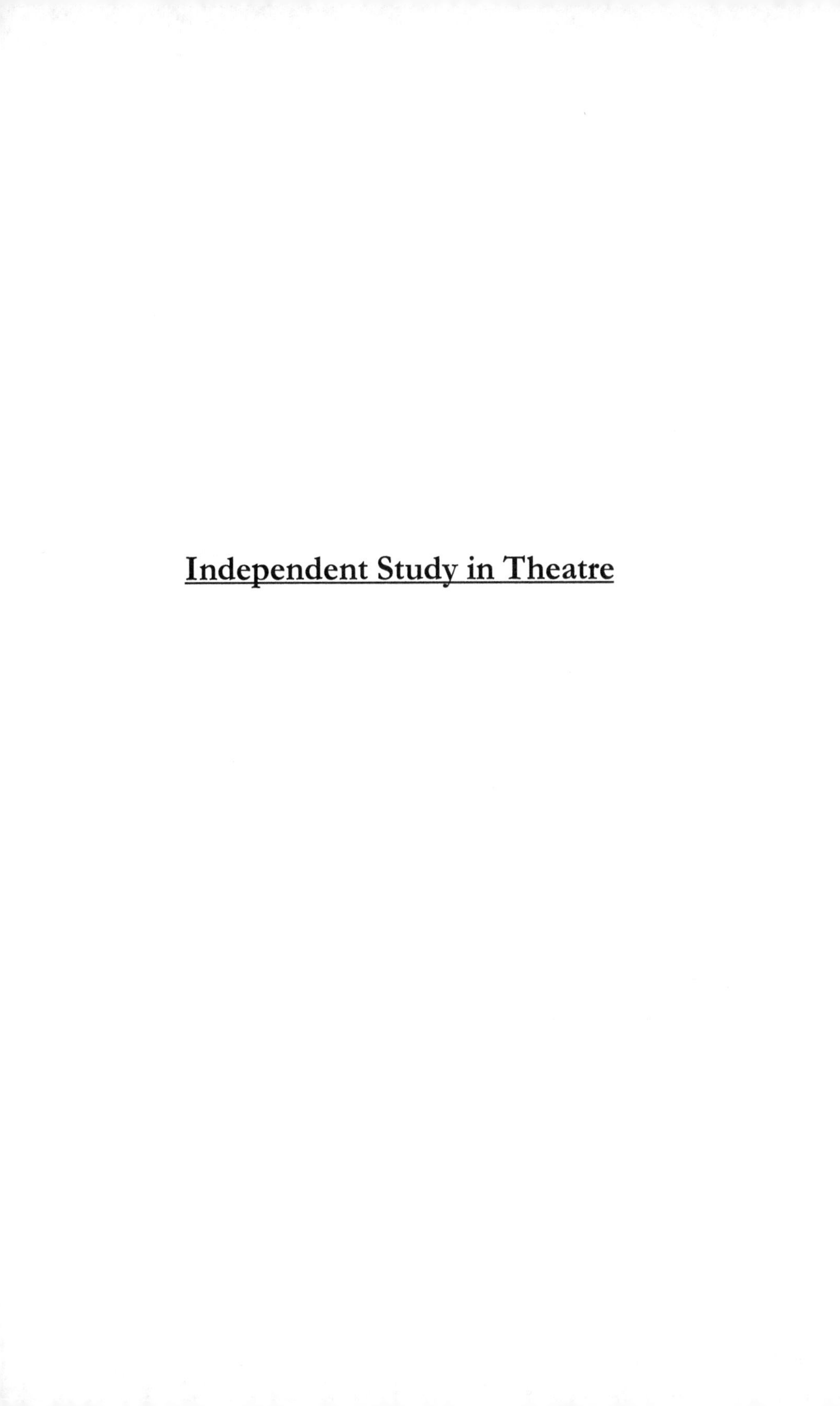

Independent Study in Theatre

About Independent Study in Theatre:

How the class works: A student submits a proposal the year before the project takes place. He chooses a faculty member as an adviser. Once the semester starts, the student and the adviser set up an in-school conference time, usually once a week, and the rehearsal work is always viewed, critiqued in progress. This generally happens after the school day.

All Independent Studies in Theatre must have research, performance and documentation of both. The performance must be viewed and will be reviewed by the advisor. In the event of that being impossible, a video must be presented as evidence of performance.

A sample of Independent Studies at Punahou School:

Directing: The Last Five Years 2014, 2009, Coser y Cantar 2013, Anthem 2012, The Actor's Nightmare, 2012 Edges, 2011, Fool for Love, 2011 On My Way, 2010, Quodlibet 2007, Durang Durang! 2006, Antigone 2006, What You Will 2005, The Great Gatsby (selected scenes) 2004

Acting: 2003 – EP, KM 2005 - LC, 2008 – EH

Stage Management: Godspell 2005 – RF, Thoroughly Modern Millie 2013 – KH, Guys and Dolls 2014 – MJ

Design: 2009 – RF
(Student initials are used here for their anonymity.)

<u>Independent Study Proposal Template</u>

<u>OBJECTIVE:</u> The primary purpose and objective of this exercise is to <u>introduce</u> to the learner to…

<u>HOW MEASURED/PROCEDURE/CLASS SYLLABUS</u>

The class meets regularly once a cycle for review, handing out of projects/monologues and submission of projects. The learner's "free time" is for rehearsal, extra sessions with his/her instructor for acting/directing sessions, organizational meetings.

<u>RESOURCES:</u> (list your bibliography here)

<u>METHODS OF EVALUATION/ASSESSMENT:</u>

Final Performance subjected to Public Critique
Journal Work
Final Paper
Graded homework
Book reports

<u>REQUIREMENTS: (These are collected and stored at the end of the semester)</u>

1)   **<u>THE JOURNAL/PORTFOLIO</u>**
2)   **<u>FINAL EVALUATIVE PAPER</u>**
3)   **<u>PUBLIC PERFORMANCE or DVD</u> of performance**

Independent Study: Acting Requirements

The Actor's Portfolio

consists of:

1. **The Course Proposal** - this is submitted early on before enrollment. The student plots a course plan, stating learning objectives, evidence of these objectives, and deadlines. The student submits evidence that these deadlines were met.

2. **A rehearsal journal.** Areas to write about may include: show concept, director's style, ensemble work, new acting techniques learned, comments about fellow actors work, problems and how they were overcome (and if they were not how a compromise was achieved).

3. **Research you did in rehearsal.** This may mean internet websites, books on costume, makeup, character portrayal, script analysis texts, books on the play you are performing.

4. **Evidence of rehearsal and performance.** These may be (but are not limited to) rehearsal photos, handouts given to the cast, scripts marked with stage directions/blocking, playbills, reviews of the show.

All this is submitted (in an organized fashion) in a one inch (or thicker) black three ring binder.

The Acting Final Paper is a 1,000-word paper that must include...

1. A summary of the learning experience that transpired while rehearsing and performing this show. The paper should refer to the experiences you documented in your rehearsal journal. It highlights moments, special experiences, learning "gems".

2. A bibliography and a list of websites that you found useful as you researched your show.

This must be submitted in the black three-ring binder that has your portfolio.

Independent Study: Design Requirements

The Final Design Portfolio
This is a final review of the entire process you went through as a designer.

Evaluate these events:
1) Pre-show meetings
2) Show concept and execution
3) Construction
4) Technical Rehearsals
5) Performances
6) Strike
7) Post Show evaluation

Hand in along with your marked designers script, renderings, model (if you made one), program of the show and any other material you see fit.

Independent Study: Stage Management Requirements

The Final Stage Manager Portfolio
This is a final review of the entire process you went through as a stage manager.

Evaluate these events:
1) Pre-show meetings
2) Auditions
3) Casting
4) Rehearsals
5) Performances
6) Strike
7) Post Show evaluation

Hand in along with your marked stage manager script, program of the show and any other material you see fit.

The Final Performance Evaluation Paper.

Review the entire process in terms of the learning experience.

Casting – the ups and downs of the people you worked with – what were some of the surprises, and possible words of advice for the next group of people who want to do the same thing? Don't name names. Try to see, now that you know what you know, how would have solved that problem person or situation.

Song choices – the decisions you made, show order, crowd response to the songs themselves. Were you ever surprised at how difficult or how easy certain pieces were? Were certain songs ones you'd never do again if you had the choice?

Did the "theme" come from the song choices, or did it come later? Is a show concept important to you in your own mind?

The Rehearsal process - Evaluate your use of time, people and how you could have better managed what you did. Were there deadlines? Was there a method in how you structured the rehearsal time? Any lessons learned?

Performance – How did you feel about what happened? More or less Performances? Should the show have been longer? Shorter? Any feedback about what and how you performed?

The final question – would you do it again? How different would it be if you did?

Hand this in with all your "show evidence" -
1) The light cue book
2) The show DVD
3) The program
4) This paper

Independent Study: Directing   2nd Semester Proposal

Proposal:

    I would like to direct/choreograph/perform in a themed musical theatre revue this spring. This would consist of 6-8 performers from the Academy and myself in the Drama Workshop, (this would be the most ideal space for this type of performance). I would hope to have at least two performances, (to evaluate improvement, compare, etc.), one evening and one day time depending on circumstance and availability in the DWS. My goal is to mount a production, with having full control of casting, organization, spectacle, etc. and to gain experience in preparation for my future in theatre.

Theme:

In conjunction with the Theatre Performance class 'run of *Twelfth Night*, I would be interested in using Love and Deception, (namely of gender), as the themes in my revue. I think it would be interesting to find songs dealing with the various aspects of love, male versus female decisions and opinions, and how gender plays a role in all of this. Depending on the cast and how many performers of each gender I can get, I would really like for people to sing numbers that are typically sung by a character of the opposite gender. However, this may not be the case if enough males are available, (due to the keys of most female numbers); it may work depending on the performers. If this does not work, then I would at least want some sort of reference to gender/deception in the songs.

Production:

I am looking to keep the overall production very simple, with minimal costume and props. I want the audience to focus on the music and talent in the revue, (not much unlike the revues put on by the American Musical Theatre Class). If we run at the same time *Twelfth Night* does, we could work with whatever set is built for the show.

Depending on the individual songs and talent that participates, I would like to have everyone sing one song, (maybe some will sing one more with some harmonization), and at least two company numbers. I would probably incorporate some dance into group numbers, if dancers are available. Each song would be preceded by a short introduction of what the number is and where it lies in the context of the show. I would hope to have an hour-long show if possible. I already have an excellent accompanist in mind; he is willing to help, so we just need to set the dates and tell him seeing how he is very busy.

Please let me know if you have any other suggestions.

    If this is approved, I will start asking people about their schedules and interest in helping me with this production. I have already begun thinking of songs, but I wanted to finalize the theme and know who will be participating before I get in over my head. I am really looking forward to doing something I've never done before.

Sincerely,

AN ACTING BIBIOGRAPHY (there are so many more, but start with these)

THE GREAT ACTING TEACHERS AND THEIR METHODS. Brestoff, Richard. Lyme, NH: Smith and Kraus, 1995. 208 pages.
Until another one comes around, this is the best book to get a feel for what the great acting teachers taught and how they taught. A must have for actors. There is a second edition, with "lesser" teachers.

ON THE TECHNIQUE OF ACTING. Chekhov, Michael. New York, New York: HarperCollins Publishers, Inc. 1991. 180 pages.
A compilation of Chekhov's "To the Actor" plus additional acting exercises makes this the best book to understand this brilliant actor's technique. One can see from reading this work how other teachers were influenced by this genius.

MAKE THEATRE HAPPEN: ACTING AND DIRECTING Palmore, Paul. Draft to Digital, 2019. 80 pages.
Series one of this book. Good stuff here! (A slight bias...)

THE TECHNIQUE OF ACTING. Adler, Stella. New York: Bantam Books,1988. 132 pages.
The acting guru, who advocates her form of Stanislavski acting. A bit simplistic, yet very useful. Forward by Marlon Brando, a student.

ON ACTING. Meisner, Sanford and Dennis Longwell. New York: Vintage Books, 1987. 254 pages.
Meisner may be the greatest acting teacher ever. This book will give you clues why that is so. A must read.

STRASBERG'S METHOD. Hull, S. Loraine. Woodbridge, Connecticut: Ox Bow Publishing, 1985. 358 pages.
A pupil of Strasberg explains his method and exercises. Strasberg is not as crazy intense as some people make him out to be. A lot of good practical stuff for the actor and teacher in here.

STAGE MAKEUP. Corson, Richard. 8th edition. Englewood Cliffs, NJ: Prentice Hall, 1989. 411 pages.
The best book on makeup ever. It keeps getting better with each edition.

<u>Voice:</u>

<u>ACCENTS</u>: A Manual for Actors. Blumenfield, Robert. New York: Limelight Editions, 2000. 317 pages.
So far, the most comprehensive accent manual. The European and British accents are quite good. Unfortunately, not so true with the Asian accent generalizations. Demonstration CD is included.

<u>FREEING THE NATURAL VOICE</u> Linklater, Kristin. New York: Drama Publishers, 1976. 211 pages.
For the longest time this was THE book on voice production. Not as much in vogue, but still a worthwhile read.

<u>VOICE AND THE ALEXANDER TECHNIQUE</u> Heirich, Jane. Berkeley, California: Mornum Time Press, 2005. 171 pages.
The latest book from the teacher of the Alexander Technique at the University of Michigan. A demonstration CD is included.

<u>THE ACTOR AND HIS TEXT</u> and **<u>VOICE AND THE ACTOR</u>** Berry, Cecily. New York: Macmillan Publishing Company, 1987 and1973.
The Royal Shakespeare Company's guru on vocal technique. The examples in the books are mostly Shakespeare pieces. Among her pupils include Jeremy Irons, Anthony Hopkins, Peter O'Toole, Richard Burton, some of the greatest voices around. She's doing something right.

Additional material by Paul D Palmore:

<u>Make Theatre Happen: Acting and Directing</u>

Coming:

<u>Make Theatre Happen III: Design</u>

All illustrations in this book are by the author using Sketchup.